D1171247

Cooking in Style

Cooking in Style

GOURMET RECIPES WITHOUT MEAT OR FISH

SONIA ALLISON

ELM TREE BOOKS : LONDON

First published in Great Britain 1980
by Elm Tree Books/Hamish Hamilton Ltd
Garden House 57-59 Long Acre London WC2E 9JZ

Illustrations by Andy Harrison

British Library Cataloguing in Publication Data

Allison, Sonia
  Cooking in style
  1. Title
  641.5-636   TX837

  ISBN 0 241 10352 5

Typeset by Pioneer
Printed in Great Britain by
Lowe & Brydone Printers Ltd, Thetford, Norfolk

Contents

The author would like to thank the following for their co-operation:
Olives from Spain
Kerrygold
Brittany Prince Vegetables and Fruits
South African Avocados
Carmel Produce
Sharwoods
Kraft Foods
Colman's Foods
Gales
Foods From France
Belgian Chicory
Cadbury
Dutch Fruit and Vegetables
Dutch Dairy Bureau

Introduction

I have no idea what you are expecting but this is not a book for food faddists, vegans, slimmers, hypochondriacs or anyone bothered by cholesterol intake. It is, in essence, a normal sort of book for normal sort of people who derive pleasure from eating good food well cooked.

My reasons for cutting out meat, fish, poultry and offal are not, I regret to say, because of conscience or morality but simply to prove to myself and others (sceptics that we all are) that one can survive deliciously on any number of dishes made from dairy products, nuts, fruits, vegetables, eggs, pasta, rice and pulses — laced here and there with the occasional dash of alcohol.

Whether you agree with me or not is another matter. All I can tell you is that I thoroughly enjoyed testing the recipes and, in turn, entertaining family and friends to three and four-course meals based on some of the dishes in the book.

One way or another, we are all connoisseurs where food is concerned. For that reason, I hope you will eat your way through the contents with as much enthusiasm as I did. Bon chance!

London, March 1978   SONIA ALLISON

Publishers' Note

The approximate metric equivalents for the spoon measures given in the recipes are:

½ teaspoon = 2.5ml
1 teaspoon = 5ml
1 dessertspoon = 10ml
1 tablespoon = 15ml

Metric measurements may vary from recipe to recipe, and it is essential to follow *either* imperial or metric measures throughout any one recipe.

Party Nibblers and Starters

Greek Zatziki Yogurt Dip — serves 4 to 6

> ½ large peeled cucumber
> 1 carton (150g/5 oz) plain yogurt
> ½ level teaspoon garlic salt
> 2 tablespoons olive oil
> 2 teaspoons lemon juice
> 1 teaspoon wine vinegar
> 1 level teaspoon sugar
> salt and pepper to taste
> 1 level tablespoon finely chopped fresh mint
> pieces of Pita bread for 'dunking'

1.   Coarsely grate the cucumber and place in a clean tea towel. Wring out until almost no liquid remains.
2.   Beat the yogurt with all remaining ingredients except the bread. Stir in the cucumber and mix well.
3.   Spoon into a small dish and sprinkle with mint. Place the dish on a large platter and surround with Pita bread (Middle Eastern style flat bread).
Note
The Zatziki is best if lightly chilled in the refrigerator before serving.

'Felafels' — serves about 6 to 8

3 rounded tablespoons burghul or cracked wheat (available from some
   Oriental stores and health food shops)
6 tablespoons boiling water
225g (8 oz) chick peas, soaked in plenty of water overnight
1 large garlic clove, crushed
1 small onion, grated
1 rounded tablespoon chopped parsley
1 level teaspoon cumin seeds (optional)
2 level tablespoons plain flour
1½ to 2 level teaspoons salt
shake of white pepper
oil for frying

1. Soak the burghul in boiling water for 20 minutes. Leave on one side temporarily.
2. Drain the chick peas. *Do not cook* but grind to a coarse mixture in a blender goblet. Spoon into a bowl. Add the burghul with all remaining ingredients except the oil. Mix thoroughly.
3. Shape into about 30 balls with damp hands. Deep fry in hot oil for 5 to 6 minutes or until golden brown and crisp. Drain on paper towels. Serve hot or cold with drinks.
Note
This is a speciality from Israel. Usually 5 or 6 Felafel are popped inside Pita bread with a salad of cucumber and tomato and sesame seed sauce, more commonly known in the country as Tahina. Available from cafes everywhere, Felafels are regarded as a complete meal. For those interested, Tahina is available canned from speciality shops in the UK.

Hummus — serves 8

2 cans (each about 400g/14 oz) chick peas, drained
2 medium garlic cloves, crushed
2 tablespoons olive oil
juice of 1 medium lemon
boiling water
salt and white pepper to taste

1. Blend the chick peas and garlic to a smooth purée in a blender goblet. Spoon into a bowl.
2. Beat in the oil, lemon juice and sufficient boiling water to make the Hummus the consistency of a thickish mayonnaise. Season to taste with salt and pepper.
3. For a traditional finish, spread into a shallow bowl and make a few indentations on the top with the back of a spoon. Fill with extra olive oil.

Sprinkle the rest of the Hummus with chopped mint. Eat with Pita bread.

Note

This is a 'classic' starter dish throughout the Balkans and Middle East.

Aubergine Cream Dip with Garlic and Herbs — serves 8

¾kg (1½ lb) aubergines
4 tablespoons lemon juice
1 packet (about 75g/3 oz) Philadelphia cream cheese with garlic and herbs
salt to taste

1. Grill the aubergines under a very high heat for about 20 minutes or until the skin is charred and the flesh feels tender when gently squeezed. Turn frequently for even cooking.
2. Rinse the aubergines under cold, running water, removing the skins at the same time. Put the aubergines into a colander. Squeeze hard against the sides to remove as much moisture as possible.
3. Transfer to a chopping board and quickly cut into pieces with a stainless knife. Place in a blender with the rest of the ingredients. Blend to a purée.
4. Spoon into a smallish serving bowl. Stand the bowl on a large dish. Surround with dunks of celery pieces, carrot slices and cauliflower florets.

Note

Instead of grilling, aubergines may be baked in moderately hot oven (220°C/400°F, Gas 6) for 20 minutes.

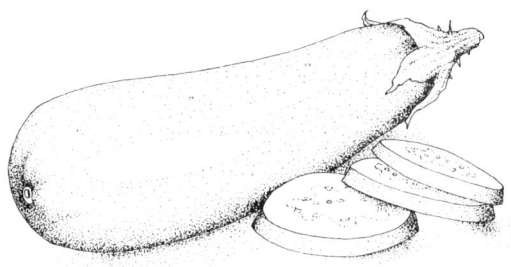

Israeli Aubergine Dip — serves 8

¾kg (1½ lb) aubergines
4 tablespoons lemon juice
1 large onion, very finely grated
2 medium blanched tomatoes, skinned and chopped
½ small red pepper, de-seeded and chopped
½ small green pepper, de-seeded and chopped

1 large garlic clove, crushed
2 tablespoons salad oil
1 to 1½ level teaspoons salt

Garnish
mint or parsley, finely chopped

1.   Grill the aubergines under a very high heat for about 20 minutes or until the skin is charred and the flesh feels tender when gently squeezed. Turn frequently for even cooking.
2.   Rinse the aubergines under cold, running water, removing the skins at the same time. Put the aubergines into a colander. Squeeze hard against the sides to remove as much moisture as possible.
3.   Transfer to a chopping board. Sprinkle with half the lemon juice. Chop finely with a stainless knife. Spoon into a bowl. Add the rest of the lemon juice with all the remaining ingredients.
4.   Mix thoroughly. Pile neatly into a serving bowl. Garnish with mint or parsley. Serve with fresh Pita bread.

'Poor Man's Caviar' — serves 8

Another Mid-East speciality, this is made exactly in the same way as the above recipe, except that the peppers are omitted. It is also eaten with Pita bread and treated as a dip.
Note
Instead of grilling, aubergines may be baked in moderately hot oven (220°C/400°F, Gas 6) for 20 minutes.

Stilton Celery Bites — serves about 8

225g (8 oz) ripe Stilton cheese
25g (1 oz) butter, softened
1 tablespoon single cream
salt and pepper to taste
8 large celery stalks, well-washed and dried

Garnish
paprika
blanched pistachio nuts, very finely chopped

1.   Beat together the Stilton cheese, butter and cream. Season to taste with salt and pepper. Add a little extra cream if the mixture is on the dry side.
2.   Spoon the Stilton 'pâté' smoothly into the celery and cut into 2½cm (1 in) lengths. Sprinkle half with paprika; half with chopped pistachios.

Italian Style Cocktail Fingers — serves about 8

> *175g (6 oz) Gorgonzola cheese*
> *25g (1 oz) butter, melted*
> *4 teaspoons double cream*
> *1 standard (size 3) egg, separated*
> *fingers of toast*

1. Mash the cheese finely. Beat in the butter, cream and egg yolk.
2. Beat the egg white to stiff snow. Fold into the cheese mixture. Spread over fingers of toast.
3. Grill until golden and puffy and serve hot.

Avocado Cream Dip — serves about 6 to 8

> *2 medium avocados*
> *2 tablespoons lemon juice*
> *150ml (¼ pt) single cream*
> *½ level teaspoon salt*
> *¼ level teaspoon garlic granules or*
> *2 garlic cloves, crushed*

1. Peel the avocados as you would peel a pear, starting from the pointed end. Cut directly into a blender goblet. Add the lemon juice. Blend to smooth purée.
2. Spoon into a bowl. Beat in the rest of the ingredients. Transfer neatly to a small, attractive serving dish. Stand in the centre of a large plate.
3. Surround with dips of smallish squares of butter-fired brown bread (cold) and pieces of Greek style Feta cheese.
Note
If Feta cheese is unavailable, use Caerphilly.

Cucumber Vol-au-Vent — serves 6 to 8

> *1 large or 2 medium cucumbers (about ½kg/1 lb)*
> *1 packet (75g/3 oz) Philadelphia cream cheese with garlic and herbs*
> *25g (1 oz) pinenuts, toasted*
> *2 small tomatoes, cut into 16 thin wedges*

1. Peel the cucumber or cucumbers thinly. Cut into 3¾cm (1½ in) lengths. Remove the inside seeds with an apple corer.
2. Fill with equal amounts of cheese then press the pinenuts on top of each to form clusters.
3. Stand on a d'oyley-lined platter. Top each 'Vol-au-Vent' with a wedge of tomato.

Pineapple and Pomegranate Cocktails — serves 8

1 large pineapple (1½kg/3 lb)
3 large pomegranates
225g (8 oz) fresh dates
4 tablespoons Cointreau

1. Peel the pineapple and remove any brown 'eyes' with an apple corer. Slice thinly. Cut the slices into triangular-shaped pieces (not too big), removing the centre core which is usually tough.
2. Transfer the pineapple triangles to a large mixing bowl. To prepare the pomegranates, cut each fruit into quarters. Bend the quarters backwards over the bowl. As you do so, you will notice that the seeds detach themselves from both the skin and inside membranes and, with a little help from your fingers, will drop into the bowl neatly and cleanly!
3. Skin the dates, remove the stones and coarsely chop the flesh. Add to the bowl with the Cointreau. Toss the fruits over and over with 2 spoons. Cover the bowl. Refrigerate for about 4 hours or until thoroughly chilled.
4. Stir round before serving.

Gingered Ogen Melons — serves 4

Halve 2 ripe Ogen melons and remove the inside seeds. Fill the hollows with ginger wine then float in some slivers of preserved ginger. Refrigerate for about 1½ to 2 hours or until cold. Serve in bowls.

Egg and Hazelnut Stuffed Avocados — serves 4

2 large avocados
1 tablespoon lemon juice

Filling
2 hardboiled eggs, finely chopped or grated
1 medium onion, finely grated
50g (2 oz) hazelnuts, ground in a blender or food processor
½ to 1 level teaspoon salt

Topping
8 rounded teaspoons soured cream
paprika

1. Halve the avocados. Remove the stones. Sprinkle the flesh with lemon juice to stop discolouration.
2. For filling, combine the eggs with the onion and hazelnuts. Season with salt. Spoon equal amounts into the avocados, smoothing it neatly.
3. Top each half with 2 teaspoons of soured cream. Sprinkle with paprika. Chill for about ½ hour before serving.

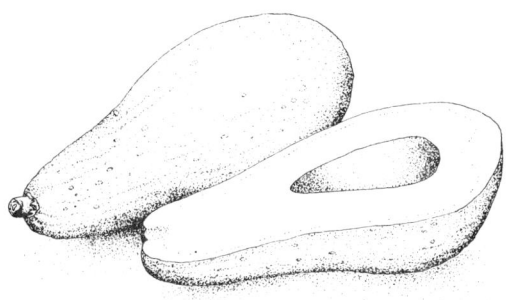

Baked Avocados à la Suisse — serves 4

75g (3 oz) fresh white or brown breadcrumbs
75g (3 oz) Emmental cheese, grated
large pinch of dried tarragon
2 large avocados
2 tablespoons lemon juice
2 level teaspoons Dijon mustard
1 standard egg, beaten
salt and pepper to taste
4 teaspoons lightly toasted breadcrumbs
25g (1 oz) butter

Garnish
12 walnut halves

1. Combine the first 3 ingredients in a mixing bowl. Halve the avocados. Remove the flesh, leaving 1¼cm (½ in) thick shells. Brush the insides of the shells with lemon juice to stop them browning.
2. Put the avocado flesh into a separate bowl. Add the rest of the lemon juice. Mash fairly finely. Add to the crumb mixture with the mustard, egg and salt and pepper to taste.
3. Mix thoroughly with a stainless fork. Pile into the avocado halves then smooth neatly with a knife.
4. Sprinkle with toasted crumbs, dot with butter and bake for 8 minutes in a hot oven preheated to 220°C/425°F, Gas 7. Stud each with walnut halves and serve straight away.

Heavenly Cocktail — serves 4

2 large grapefruit
2 large oranges
125g (4 oz) fresh dates
1 medium avocado

7

1.   Peel the grapefruit and oranges, removing all traces of pith. With hands held over a bowl to catch juices, cut out segments of fruit from in between the membranes. Allow to fall into the bowl.

2.   Slide the skins off the dates and discard. Split lengthwise. Remove the stones. Peel the avocado as you would peel a pear, starting from the pointed end. Dice the flesh with a stainless knife.

3.   Add the dates and avocado to the bowl containing the grapefruit and oranges. Toss gently to mix. Cover. Chill for 1 hour.

4.   Just before serving, divide between 4 stemmed glasses. Accompany with teaspoons for easy eating.

Dressed Mushrooms — serves 4

> *½kg (1 lb) mushrooms*
> *6 tablespoons olive oil (necessary for flavour)*
> *3 large garlic cloves, crushed*
> *1 level teaspoon dry mustard*
> *½ level teaspoon salt*
> *1 teaspoon Worcester sauce*
> *1 level teaspoon marjoram*
> *2 tablespoons cider vinegar*
> *parsley for garnishing, finely chopped*

1.   Wash and dry the mushrooms and peel if necessary. Remove the stalks and chop coarsely. Place in a bowl. Thinly slice the mushrooms. Add to the bowl.

2.   To make the dressing, beat the oil with the next 6 ingredients. Pour into the bowl over the mushrooms and stalks.

3.   Toss thoroughly. Spoon into 4 dishes. Sprinkle each heavily with parsley. Serve straight away.

Note

The portions are generous and will stretch easily to 6 servings.

Avocados with Nutty Yogurt Sauce — serves 4

> *150g (about 5 oz) plain yogurt*
> *1 large garlic clove, crushed*
> *25g (1 oz) ground hazelnuts*
> *1 slightly rounded tablespoon thick mayonnaise*
> *1 large hard boiled egg, grated*
> *salt and pepper to taste*
> *2 large avocados*
> *lemon juice*

1.   Spoon the yogurt into a bowl. Add the next 4 ingredients. Mix well.

Season to taste with salt and pepper.
2.   Halve the avocados and brush with lemon juice to stop them browning. Fill the centres with the yogurt mixture. Serve straight away.

Artichokes with Tangy Tomato Mayonnaise — serves 6

> *6 large artichokes*
> *4 rounded tablespoons thick mayonnaise*
> *1 medium garlic clove, crushed*
> *1 tablespoon tubed or canned tomato concentrate*
> *2 teaspoons Worcester sauce*

1.   Cut the stems off the artichokes then remove the first two rows of leaves (nearest to stem). These are often damaged and also tough.
2.   Place, nose sides down, in cold salted water. Leave to soak for ½ hour. Drain and shake out surplus water.
3.   Stand the artichokes, in an upright position, in 1 large saucepan or 2 smaller ones. Add about 7½cm (3 in) water and 1½ level teaspoons salt to the pan (or pans).
4.   Bring to the boil. Lower heat. Cover. Simmer gently for about 40 to 50 minutes or until tender and you can tell when by pulling out a leaf. If it comes away easily, then the artichokes have been cooked for long enough.
5.   Drain thoroughly. To serve you can do one of three things. Either serve hot with suitable dressing; serve cold with suitable dressing; lift out the cone of leaves in the centre, remove the furry choke carefully and fill the hollow with a suitable dressing when cold.
6.   To make the tangy tomato dressing, combine the mayonnaise with all the remaining ingredients. Serve with the cold artichokes, either separately or inside hollows.
Note
To eat, pull off a leaf at a time and dip the pale green end in the dressing. Pass between the teeth. Continue in this way until you reach the furry choke (unless it has been removed already). Carefully remove it with your knife, then smother the heart with dressing and eat it with a knife and fork.

Artichokes with Pepper and Garlic Butter — serves 6

Cook the artichokes as directed in the recipe for Artichokes with Tangy Tomato Mayonnaise. Serve hot (without removing the centres) with Pepper and Garlic Butter made by melting 175g (6 oz) butter and adding to it the following:

> *4 rounded teaspoons canned green peppers (Poivre Vert de Madagascar)*
> *½ level teaspoon garlic granules*
> *salt and freshly milled pepper to taste*

Artichokes with Summer Curd Cheese Dressing — serves 6

Cook the artichokes as directed in the recipe for Artichokes with Tangy Tomato Mayonnaise. Serve cold with the following dressing used to fill the hollows: mix 225g (8 oz) curd cheese with 4 tablespoons milk, 1 level tablespoon scissor-snipped chives, ½ level tablespoon finely chopped mint, ½ level teaspoon salt and ½ level teaspoon paprika.

Winter Sunshine Cocktail with Madeira — serves 2

> *4 medium grapefruits*
> *4 medium pomegranates*
> *2 tablespoons Madeira*

1. Peel the grapefruit, removing all traces of pith. Using a sharp knife, cut out the flesh from in between the membranes. Do this over a bowl so that the segments of fruit and juice fall directly into it.
2. To prepare the pomegranates, cut each fruit into quarters. Bend the quarters backwards over the bowl. The seeds, with a bit of help from your fingers, will come away from skin etc very easily.
3. Add the Madeira to the fruit and toss well with 2 spoons. Cover and chill for at least 2 hours in the refrigerator. To serve, spoon equal amounts into 6 bowls.

Palm Heart and Brazil Nut Cocktail — serves 4

> *8 lettuce leaves*
> *1 can (about 425g/15 oz) hearts of palm in natural juice, drained*
> *50g (2 oz) Brazil nuts, sliced*
> *1 medium garlic clove, crushed*
> *2 rounded tablespoons thick mayonnaise*
> *1 rounded tablespoon chopped parsley*
> *paprika*

1. Wash and dry the lettuce leaves. Use to cover 4 medium sized plates. Cut the palm hearts into 1½cm (½ in) thick slices. Place in a mixing bowl.
2. Add the nuts, garlic and mayonnaise. Toss well to mix. Spoon equal amounts over lettuce. Sprinkle with parsley and paprika.

Hot and Cold Soups

Farmhouse Split Pea Soup — serves 4 to 6

225g (8 oz) yellow split peas, soaked overnight
1¼l (2 pt) water
3 level teaspoons salt
225g (8 oz) parsnips, diced
225g (8 oz) onions, chopped
225g (8 oz) potatoes, grated
175g (6 oz) carrots, thinly sliced

1.   Drain the peas. Place in a sturdy pan with water and salt. Add all the prepared vegetables except the carrots.
2.   Bring to the boil, stirring. Lower heat. Cover. Simmer for 1¾ hours, stirring occasionally as soup is inclined to catch. If it seems to be thickening-up too much, add a little boiling water.
3.   Add the carrot slices and continue to cook a further ¼ hour. Adjust seasoning to taste and serve piping hot.

Italian 'Lace' Soup — serves 4 to 6

⅞l (1½ pt) onion water (left over from boiling onions)
2 standard eggs
50g (2 oz) grated Parmesan cheese
2 level tablespoons fine semolina
salt and pepper to taste

1.   Pour the onion water into a saucepan. Bring to the boil. Beat together the eggs, cheese and semolina.
2.   Trickle, from a height, into the soup, whisking all the time.
3.   Bring the soup back to the boil, season to taste and ladle into 4 or 6 soup plates or bowls. If liked, sprinkle lightly with extra Parmesan cheese.
Note
When the soup comes to the boil, it will take on a curdled appearance and look somewhat like lace — hence its name.

Russian-Style Cabbage Soup — serves 6

1½l (2½ pt) water
1kg (2 lb) white cabbage, finely shredded
225g (8 oz) onions, chopped
½kg (1 lb) blanched tomatoes, skinned and chopped
3 level teaspoons salt
150ml (¼ pt) soured cream
150g (5 oz) yogurt
freshly milled pepper to taste

To serve
rye bread and butter

1.   Place all the ingredients, except the last 3, into large pan. Bring to the boil, stirring.
2.   Lower heat and cover. Simmer gently for 1 hour, stirring occasionally. Whisk in the soured cream and yogurt. Season with pepper. Reheat briefly.
3.   Ladle into warm soup plates or bowls and serve with rye bread and butter.

Butter Bean Broth — serves 6 to 8

225g (8 oz) haricot beans, soaked overnight
1½l (2½ pt) water
2 large carrots, sliced
175g (6 oz) onion, chopped
1 large and trimmed leek, well-washed and sliced
175g (6 oz) swede, diced

225g (8 oz) potatoes, diced
3 large celery stalks, thinly sliced
3 level teaspoons salt
2 heaped tablespoons chopped parsley

1.   Drain the beans. Place in a large pan with water. Bring to the boil and skim. Lower heat and cover pan. Simmer for 1 to 1¼ hours or until the beans are almost tender.
2.   Add all the remaining ingredients except the parsley. Bring to the boil again. Cover. Cook gently for about ¾ hour, stirring from time to time.
3.   Ladle into 6 or 8 large soup plates and sprinkle with parsley.

Lettuce Cream Soup — serves 6

Follow the recipe for the Lettuce Cream given in the recipe for Chilli Beans and Chick Peas with Lettuce Cream on page 00. When the lettuce cream is finished, whisk in 275ml (½ pt) water. Adjust seasoning to taste. Reheat until hot. Ladle into soup cups or bowls.

Courtly Cream of Mustard Soup — serves 4 to 6

2 large onions, peeled but left whole
1l (1¾ pt) water
2 level teaspoons salt
50g (2 oz) butter
50g (2 oz) plain flour
275ml (½ pt) milk
2 egg yolks
4 tablespoons double cream
3 level tablespoons Meaux mustard
extra salt and white pepper to taste

Garnish
Chopped watercress

1.   Cook the onions in water and salt for about 30 to 40 minutes to extract as much flavour as possible. Drain, reserving 575ml (1 pt) of the onion water. (Keep the onions as well and use in cooking.)
2.   Melt the butter in a clean pan. Stir in the flour. Cook for 2 minutes without browning. Gradually blend in the onion water and milk. Cook, stirring, until the soup comes to the boil and thickens. Cover. Simmer for 10 minutes.
3.   Beat the egg yolks and cream well together. Stir in 6 tablespoons of the hot soup. Pour back into the pan of soup. Stir round and remove from the heat. Whisk in the mustard.

4. Adjust seasoning to taste. Ladle the soup into 4 or 6 soup plates. Sprinkle each with watercress. Serve straight away.

French Onion Soup — serves 6

½kg (1 lb) onions
50g (2 oz) butter
2 teaspoons olive oil
1½ level tablespoons flour
1¼l (2 pt) hot water
salt and freshly milled black pepper to taste
6 slices French bread, cut diagonally
extra butter
175g (6 oz) Gruyère or Emmental cheese

1. Peel the onions and cut into wafer-thin slices. Heat the butter and oil in a large, heavy-based pan. Add the onions.
2. Fry gently, with the lid on the pan, until they turn a deep gold. Stir in the flour. Gradually blend in the hot water.
3. Bring to the boil, stirring continuously all the time. Simmer gently for ½ hour. Season to taste with salt and pepper then pour the soup into a medium-sized tureen. Top with buttered bread slices then sprinkle heavily with the grated cheese.
4. Heat until the cheese is golden and bubbly for about 10 to 15 minutes in hot oven set to 220°C/425°F, Gas 7.
5. Remove from the oven and ladle into 6 individual soup bowls. Serve while still very hot.
Note
For a speedier end to the soup, spread the bread evenly with butter then cover each slice thickly with grated cheese. Brown under a hot grill. Ladle the soup into bowls, place a slice of toasted cheese bread in each.

Spinach Chowder — serves 6

50g (2 oz) butter
50g (2 oz) plain flour
575ml (1 pt) milk
150ml (¼ pt) single cream
150ml (¼ pt) water
1 packet (about 300g/11 oz) frozen chopped spinach
225g (8 oz) cold cooked potatoes, diced
125g (4 oz) cold cooked carrots, diced
125g (4 oz) cooked sweetcorn
3 hard boiled eggs, coarsely chopped

¼ level teaspoon grated nutmeg
salt and pepper to taste

1. Melt the butter in a pan. Add flour. Cook, stirring, for 2 minutes, but do not allow the mixture to brown. Gradually blend in the milk, cream and water.
2. Cook, stirring continuously, until the soup comes to boil and thickens.
3. Add the block of spinach and keep stirring over lowish heat until it has completely thawed.
4. Stir in all the remaining ingredients and heat the chowder until steaming hot.
5. Ladle into deepish soup bowls or plates and serve, as a complete meal, with fresh brown rolls or hot, buttered crumpets.

Potato and Leek Soup — serves 6

¾kg (1½ lb) potatoes, coarsely chopped
4 medium trimmed leeks, slit and well washed
1¼l (2 pt) water
1½ level teaspoon salt
275ml (½ pt) single cream
3 heaped tablespoons finely chopped parsley

1. Place the potatoes into a pan. Chop the leeks and add to the pan with water and salt.
2. Bring to the boil and cover. Lower heat. Simmer until the vegetables are very soft. Blend, in 2 or 3 batches, in a blender goblet until smooth.
3. Spoon into a clean pan then gently whisk in the cream.
4. Adjust seasoning to taste (the soup might need extra salt and a sprinkling or two of pepper) and reheat until boiling. Ladle into soup bowls or cups and sprinkle each with parsley.

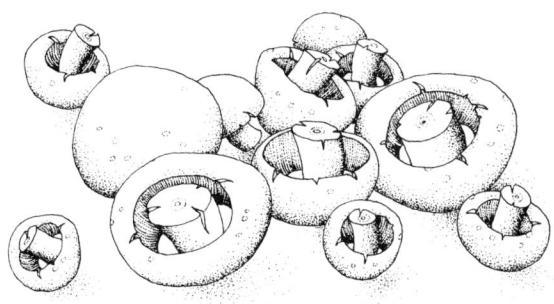

Quickie Mushroom Foam Soup — serves 4 to 6

25g (1 oz) butter

225g (8 oz) mushrooms, trimmed and sliced
2 level tablespoons flour
575ml (1 pt) milk
150ml (¼ pt) water
salt and pepper to taste
large pinch of ground nutmeg
2 standard (size 3) eggs, separated

1.   Melt the butter in a pan. When hot and sizzling, add mushrooms. Fry for 3 minutes. Stir in the flour.
2.   Cook for about 2 minutes then gradually blend in milk and water.
3.   Cook, stirring continuously, until the soup comes to the boil and thickens. Add salt and pepper to taste, the ground nutmeg and egg yolks. Whisk gently until the egg yolks are well amalgamated into the mixture.
4.   Beat the egg whites to a stiff snow. Remove the soup from the heat. Gently whisk the whites into the soup. Ladle into soup bowls or cups and serve straight away.

Fresh Tomato Soup with Sherry — serves 6 to 8

¾kg (1½ lb) blanched tomatoes, skinned and chopped
225g (8 oz) onions, chopped
575ml (1 pt) water
2 level teaspoons salt
2 level teaspoons brown sugar
2 teaspoons Worcester sauce
3 level tablespoons tubed or canned tomato concentrate
1 level teaspoon paprika
2 slightly rounded teaspoons cornflour
150ml (¼ pt) milk
about ¾ tablespoon medium sherry

1.   Place all the ingredients, except the last three, into a large and heavy-based pan.
2.   Bring slowly to the boil, stirring. Lower the heat and cover the pan. Simmer gently for 1 hour.
3.   Mix the cornflour to a smooth cream with the milk. Pour into the soup.
4.   Cook, stirring all the time, until it comes to the boil and thickens slightly. Adjust seasoning to taste. Ladle into warm soup bowls or plates and add the sherry. Serve hot with cheese straws.
Note
For a more tangy soup with a spicier flavour, add 1 bay leaf and a blade of mace while the soup is cooking. Remove before serving.

Snow Cream Tomato Soup — serves 6 to 8

To vary the above recipe, blend the soup, in 2 or 3 batches, to a smooth liquid in a blender goblet. Return to the saucepan. Reheat until bubbling. Ladle into soup plates or bowls, stir sherry into each then top with mounds of softly whipped cream (about 6 tablespoons) into which the stiffly beaten white of 1 egg has been folded.

Chilled Curried Avocado Soup — serves 6

2 medium avocados
1 tablespoon lemon juice
1 carton (150g/about 5 oz) plain yogurt
1 carton (150ml/¼ pt) soured cream
6 level teaspoons mild curry powder
575ml (1 pt) chilled milk
1½ level teaspoons salt

Garnish
turmeric

1.   Peel the avocados as you would peel a pear, starting at the pointed end. Cut directly into a blender goblet. Add the next 4 ingredients. Blend until completely smooth.
2.   Spoon into a bowl. Gradually whisk in the milk and continue whisking until soup is absolutely smooth. Season with salt.
3.   Pour into 6 soup cups or plates and sprinkle each lightly with turmeric. Serve straightaway as soup tends to discolour slightly if left to stand.

Turnip Cream Soup — serves 6

½kg (1 lb) turnips, peeled and diced
½kg (1 lb) potatoes, sliced
225g (8 oz) onions, chopped
575ml (1 pt) water
3 level teaspoons salt
150ml (¼ pt) single cream
150ml (¼ pt) milk

Garnish
6 heaped teaspoons cooked peas
small croûtons of butter-fried bread

1.   Place the prepared vegetables into a large pan with water. Add salt. Bring to the boil. Cover. Simmer until the vegetables are very soft. Leave to cool to lukewarm.

2. Blend, in 4 or 6 batches, in a blender goblet until smooth and purée-like. Return to a clean pan.

3. Reheat to boiling. Stir in the cream and milk. Keep the soup over a medium heat until it bubbles. Ladle into a soup tureen or into 6 warm soup plates or bowls. Add the peas and a sprinkling of croûtons to each.

Carefree Vichyssoise — serves 8

1¼l (2 pt) onion water (water left over from boiling onions)
1 large packet instant mash (6 servings)
2 level teaspoons onion salt
275ml (½ pt) double cream

Garnish
scissor-snipped chives

1. Bring the onion water up to the boil. Tip the potato powder into a large bowl. Gradually whisk in the onion water. Season with salt. Cover and leave until completely cold.

2. Refrigerate for 4 to 5 hours. Before serving, very carefully whisk in the cream. When completely smooth, pour into individual soup bowls or cups. Sprinkle with chives.

Note

I have given a large quantity here as this chilled soup is particularly good for party entertaining.

Chilled Tomato Consommé with Drambuie — serves 6

3 level teaspoons gelatine
2 tablespoons cold water
2 tablespoons hot water
¾kg (1½ lb) tomatoes, blanched and skinned
shake of Tabasco
1 teaspoon Worcester sauce
1 level teaspoon onion powder
1 to 1½ level teaspoons salt
2 tablespoons Drambuie

Garnish
6 lemon wedges
6 small sprigs of watercress

1. Soften the gelatine for 5 minutes in the cold water. Spoon into a saucepan. Add hot water. Stir over a low heat until dissolved but do not allow to boil.

2. Blend the tomatoes until smooth in a blender goblet with all the remaining ingredients.
3. Stir in the gelatine. Cover. Refrigerate until lightly set and very cold. Break up with a fork and transfer to 6 bowls. Garnish each with a lemon wedge and watercress sprig.

Chilled Beetroot Soup — serves 8

¾kg (1½ lb) cooked beetroots
½kg (1 lb) tomatoes, blanched and skinned
2 to 3 level teaspoons salt
575ml (1 pt) cold water
1 small onion
2 medium garlic cloves
1 tablespoon malt vinegar
8 heaped teaspoons soured cream

1. Coarsely chop the beetroots and tomatoes. Blend, in two batches, with all the remaining ingredients except the cream.
2. Pour into a bowl and cover. Refrigerate for about 4 hours or until thoroughly chilled.
3. To serve, stir round and ladle into soup bowls. Top each with a teaspoon of soured cream.

Bulgarian Yogurt and Cucumber Soup — serves 8

1kg (2 lb) tub plain yogurt
2 medium cucumbers, peeled
275ml (½ pt) water
2 medium garlic cloves, crushed (essential!)
2 level teaspoons each salt and caster sugar
3 heaped tablespoons finely chopped parsley or fresh dill
8 rounded teaspoons finely chopped walnuts

1. Tip the yogurt into a bowl. Grate the cucumber into thin slices. Drain off the water by squeezing the cucumber between your hands.

2. Add to the yogurt with all the remaining ingredients except the parsley and walnuts. Stir well to mix. Cover. Chill in the refrigerator for about 4 hours.

3. Before serving, stir round and ladle into 8 soup bowls. Sprinkle each with parsley or dill and walnuts.

Chilled Tomato Cream Soup — serves 10 to 12

> *1½kg (3 lb) tomatoes, blanched and skinned*
> *2 large garlic cloves*
> *1 medium red pepper, halved and de-seeded*
> *225g (8 oz/1 large packet) Philadelphia cream cheese*
> *a handful of parsley (minus stalks)*
> *2 level teaspoons salt*
> *2 teaspoons Worcester sauce*
> *1 tablespoon malt vinegar*

1. Halve the tomatoes if large. Blend, with next 4 ingredients, in 2 batches in a blender goblet. (If the blender is small, you may need to do this in 3 or 4 batches). The mixture should be smooth.

2. Tip into a large bowl. Whisk in the rest of the ingredients. Cover. Chill in the refrigerator for at least 4 hours.

3. Before serving, stir round and ladle into soup bowls or cups. Add an ice cube to each.

Gazpacho — serves 4

> *1 large garlic clove*
> *½ medium sized green pepper, de-seeded and coarsely cut-up*
> *½ medium sized red pepper, de-seeded and coarsely cut-up*
> *½kg (1 lb) blanched tomatoes, skinned and coarsely chopped*
> *1 medium onion, cut up into pieces*
> *3 level tablespoons tubed or canned tomato concentrate*
> *2 level teaspoons caster sugar*
> *3 tablespoons olive oil*
> *2 tablespoons wine vinegar*
> *fresh crumbs from 2 large slices white bread*
> *275ml (½ pt) cold water*
> *salt and pepper to taste*

> **To accompany**
> *Bowls of:*
> *chopped cucumber*

mixture of finely chopped red and green pepper
chopped onion
hard boiled egg
fried bread cubes (tiny and fried in olive oil)

1.   Blend the first 5 ingredients in a blender goblet until smooth. Pour into a bowl. Whisk in the tomato concentrate and sugar. Stir in all the remaining ingredients.
2.   Cover. Refrigerate for about 6 hours or overnight. Before serving, stir round and ladle into bowls. Serve with suggested accompaniments to which people help themselves.

Chilled Mixed Fruit Soup — serves 8

2 cartons frozen concentrated orange juice (each ¾l or 1¼ pints)
1l (1¾ pt) water
125g (4 oz) granulated sugar
75g (3 oz) seedless raisins
1 large dessert pear, peeled and diced (core removed)
1 large eating apple, peeled and diced (core removed)
2 large oranges, peeled and chopped
1 small and ripe melon, de-seeded and flesh diced
1½ level tablespoons cornflour
3 tablespoons cold water

1.   Spoon the concentrated orange juice into a pan. Add water. Bring to the boil. Add the sugar. Stir over a low heat until dissolved.
2.   Add the next 5 ingredients. Cover the pan. Simmer gently for 45 minutes. Stir occasionally as the soup easily catches over the base of pan.
3.   To thicken, mix the cornflour to a smooth cream with water. Pour into the soup. Cook, stirring continuously, until the soup comes to the boil. Simmer for 5 minutes.
4.   Pour into a large bowl. Cool. Cover. Refrigerate until thoroughly chilled. Before serving, stir round and ladle into 8 soup plates or bowls.

Lunch Dishes

Marrow and Onion Cheese — serves 4

> *1kg (2 lb) peeled marrow, de-seeded and diced*
> *275ml (½ pt) marrow water*
> *275ml (½ pt) milk*
> *50g (2 oz) butter*
> *1 medium onion, finely grated*
> *40g (1½ oz) flour*
> *175g (6 oz) Gouda cheese, grated*
> *1 level teaspoon German mustard*
> *salt and pepper to taste*

1. Cook the marrow for 10 minutes in boiling salted water, keeping the lid on the pan throughout. Drain, reserving 275ml/½ pt of the marrow water. Combine with the milk and leave on one side temporarily.
2. Melt the butter in a fairly large pan. Add the onion. Fry gently for about 10 minutes or until pale gold.
3. Stir in the flour then gradually blend in the marrow water and milk mixture. Cook, stirring continuously, until sauce comes to the boil and

thickens. Add two-thirds of the cheese, marrow and mustard. Season to taste with salt and pepper.

4. Heat through for about 5 minutes then transfer to well-buttered casserole. Sprinkle the rest of cheese on top and brown under a hot grill.

5. Serve with baked jacket potatoes, split open and topped with plenty of butter. Grated carrots, tossed with lemon juice and salt and pepper to taste, make an excellent accompaniment.

Spaghetti with Mushroom and Olive Sauce — serves 4

5 tablespoons olive oil
½kg (1 lb) mushrooms, trimmed and sliced
175g (6 oz) onion, chopped
2 garlic cloves, crushed
12 Spanish stuffed olives, sliced
1 to 1½ level teaspoons salt
pepper to taste
350g (12 oz) (raw weight) spaghetti, freshly cooked
4 rounded tablespoons chopped parsley

1. Heat the oil in a heavy pan. Add the mushrooms, onion and garlic. Simmer gently for about ¼ hour. Stir in the olives. Season to taste with salt and pepper.

2. Drain the spaghetti thoroughly. Place in a deep bowl. Add the mushroom mixture. Toss well.

3. Divide equally between 4 warm dinner plates. Sprinkle each serving with parsley.

Stuffed Peaches Miramar — serves 4

8 lettuce leaves from round lettuces, washed and dried
4 large peaches
lemon juice
125g (4 oz) cottage cheese
½ dessert apple, washed and chopped
1 medium celery stalk, chopped
15g (½ oz) walnuts, finely chopped
1 level tablespoon very finely grated onion

Topping
canned or bottled cranberry sauce

1. Arrange the leaves over 4 bread and butter plates. Wash and dry the peaches. Cut in half. Remove stones. Sprinkle the flesh with lemon juice to stop browning.

2. Combine the cottage cheese with the rest of the ingredients. Mix well. Spoon equal amounts into the peach halves.

3. Transfer to plates — two halves on each — then top with blobs of cranberry sauce. Slimmers can eat this dish, as it is, for a special treat!

Golden Cheese and Leek Puffs — serves 4

> *1 large packet (about 400g/14 oz) frozen puff pastry, thawed*
> *50g (2 oz) butter*
> *225g (8 oz) trimmed leeks, slit and well washed*
> *25g (1 oz) flour*
> *150ml (¼ pt) single cream*
> *75g (3 oz) Lancashire cheese, crumbled*
> *salt and pepper to taste*
> *a little beaten egg for brushing*

1. Roll out the pastry fairly thinly on floured surface. Cut into 8 x 15cm (6 in) squares. Leave on one side temporarily.

2. For the filling, melt the butter in a saucepan. Add sliced leeks. Fry very slowly until pale gold, allowing about 15 minutes and keeping the pan covered throughout.

3. Stir in the flour and cook for 1 minute. Gradually blend in the cream. Cook, stirring continuously, until the mixture comes to the boil and thickens. Remove from the heat.

4. Add the cheese. Stir until melted then season well to taste. Leave on one side until cold.

5. Place equal amounts on to the centres of the pastry squares and then moisten the edges of the pastry with water. Fold over and seal securely by pinching the edges together.

6. Ridge the edges of each Puff with a fork.

7. Stand on a well-buttered baking tray and brush with beaten egg. Bake for 15/20 minutes in a hot oven set to 220°C/425°F, Gas 7. Serve hot with grilled or fried tomatoes and creamed spinach. Alternatively, serve cold with a mixed salad.

Upside Down Tomato Pudding — serves 4

> *1 can (about ½kg/1 lb) tomatoes*
> *1 level teaspoon basil*
> *225g (8 oz) self raising flour*
> *1 level teaspoon salt*
> *1 level teaspoon dry mustard*
> *125g (4 oz) butter*
> *125g (4 oz) Gouda cheese, grated*
> *2 standard (size 3) eggs*

4 tablespoons milk
1 or 2 shakes Tabasco

1. Set the oven to moderately hot, 190°C/375°F, Gas 5. Well butter a 1¼l (2 pt) pie dish. Drain the tomatoes, reserving all the juice. Arrange the tomatoes over the base of the buttered dish, crushing them down with a fork. Sprinkle with basil.
2. Sift the flour, salt and mustard into a bowl. Rub in the butter finely. Toss in the grated cheese. Using a fork, mix to a fairly stiff batter with the unbeaten eggs, milk and Tabasco.
3. Stir briskly without beating then spread the mixture smoothly over the tomatoes.
4. Bake for 1/1¼ hours when the pudding should be well risen and golden. Invert on to a plate, cut into wedges and serve with the tomato juice (heated until hot), well seasoned with salt and pepper. Accompany with green vegetables or a salad to taste.

Tangy Creamed Beets with Omelet Strips — serves 4

1 carton (150ml/¼ pt) soured cream
½ level teaspoon salt
½ level teaspoon prepared mustard
2 level teaspoons caster sugar
½kg (1 lb) pickled beetroots (drained weight), diced
6 spring onions, trimmed and chopped
1 or 2 omelets, made with 4 eggs

1. Tip the soured cream into a saucepan. Add the salt, mustard and sugar. Heat over a low heat until hot, stirring all the time.
2. Add the beetroot dice and spring onions. Heat through until hot. Pile into a serving dish. Top with the omelet or omelets, cut into thin strips.
3. Serve straight away with brown rice and a salad to taste.

Gnocchi Romana — serves 4

575ml (1 pt) milk
150g (5 oz) semolina
1 level teaspoon salt
1 standard egg, beaten
75g (3 oz) butter
75g (3 oz) grated Parmesan cheese
¼ level teaspoon nutmeg
white pepper to taste

1. Pour the milk into a heavy-based saucepan. Add the semolina and salt. Slowly bring to the boil, stirring continuously.
2. Cook gently for 5/7 minutes or until the mixture is *very thick*. Stir frequently to prevent burning.
3. Remove from the heat then beat in the egg, 50g (2 oz) butter, 50g (2 oz) cheese, nutmeg and pepper to taste.
4. Return to the heat and cook gently, stirring all the time, for 5 minutes.
5. Rinse a shallow tin measuring about 27½cm x 20cm (11 x 8 in) with cold water. *Do not wipe dry.*
6. Spread the semolina mixture into it, smoothing the top with a damp knife. Leave until cold then refrigerate until very firm.
7. Cut into 3¾cm (1½ in) squares.
8. Arrange, in overlapping circles, in a round and shallow buttered heatproof dish.
9. Sprinkle the rest of cheese on top then add flakes of butter.
10. Cook until brown and bubbling for about 15/20 minutes in moderately hot oven set to 200°C/400°F, Gas 6.
11. Spoon out of the dish and serve hot with green vegetables to taste or a salad.

Gnocchi Florentine — serves 4

Make Gnocchi exactly as directed in above recipe but arrange the squares over a bed of creamed spinach, made by blending one large can of chopped spinach (thoroughly drained) with 150ml (¼ pt) single cream and salt and pepper to taste. Complete cooking as directed in Gnocchi Romana.

Egg Scramble Grandmère — serves 4

> *3 large slices white or brown bread*
> *50g (2 oz) butter*
> *1 teaspoon salad oil*
> *8 large eggs*
> *8 tablespoons milk*
> *salt and pepper to taste*

1. Cut the bread into small dice. Fry in the butter and oil until golden brown and crisp all over.
2. Remove from pan and drain on paper towels.
3. Beat the eggs thoroughly with the rest of the ingredients. Add the fried bread cubes.
4. Pour into heavy-based saucepan. Stir and scramble gently over a low heat until the eggs are just set.
5. Divide equally between 4 plates. Serve with mange tout and a mixed salad.

Creamy Parsnip Puff — serves 4

¾kg (1½ lb) parsnips, peeled and cut up into pieces
boiling salted water
50g (2 oz) butter
2 standard (size 3) eggs, separated
1 garlic clove, crushed
1 large pinch ground mace
1 level teaspoon prepared mustard
salt and pepper to taste
125g (4 oz) mature Cheddar cheese, crumbled

1.   Well butter a 1¼l (2 pt) heatproof dish. Cook the parsnips in boiling salted water until *very* soft. Drain thoroughly and return to the saucepan.
2.   Leave over a low heat. Set oven to moderately hot, 200°C/400°F, Gas 6.
3.   Mash the parsnips finely then beat in the butter, egg yolks, garlic, mace and mustard.
4.   Season well to taste with salt and pepper. Mix well. Fold in the egg whites, first beaten to a stiff snow. Transfer to a prepared dish.
5.   Cover the top thickly with cheese, then heat through in the oven until golden brown, allowing about 25/30 minutes. Serve with baked jacket potatoes topped with sour cream, and sliced carrots tossed in butter.

Sesame Cheese Pinwheels — serves 4

225g (4 oz) self raising flour
½ level teaspoon salt
50g (2 oz) butter
7/8 tablespoons cold milk
175g (6 oz) mature Cheddar cheese, grated
1 standard egg, beaten
1 level teaspoon Meaux mustard
pinch of Cayenne pepper

Topping
beaten egg for brushing
about 4 teaspoons sesame seeds

1.   Set the oven to hot, 220°C/425°F, Gas 7. Well-butter one large baking tray.
2.   Sift the flour and salt into a bowl. Rub in the butter finely. Mix to a softish dough with the cold milk.
3.   Turn out on to a lightly floured surface. Knead quickly until smooth.
4.   Roll into an oblong measuring 27½cm x 22½cm (11 x 9 in). Cover, to within 1¼cm (½ in) of the edges, with cheese combined with all the

remaining ingredients except the beaten egg for brushing and the sesame seeds.

5. Moisten the edges with water then roll up like a Swiss roll, starting from one of the longer sides.

6. Press the edges and joins well together to seal. Cut the roll into 8 thick slices.

7. Place on buttered tray and brush with beaten egg. Sprinkle with sesame seeds, then bake for 15/20 minutes or until well-risen and golden brown. Serve hot with hard boiled eggs and tomatoes. If liked, the pinwheels may be spread with butter.

Devilled Buck Rarebits — serves 4

> *4 slices white or brown bread*
> *25g (1 oz) butter, softened*
> *125g (4 oz) mature Cheddar cheese, grated*
> *1 teaspoon tomato ketchup*
> *1 teaspoon Worcester sauce*
> *½ level teaspoon dry mustard*
> *1 level teaspoon curry powder*
> *shake of Tabasco*
> *4 freshly fried eggs*

1. Toast the bread on one side only. Mix the butter to a paste with all the remaining ingredients (except the eggs).

2. Spread over the untoasted sides of the bread and brown under a hot grill. Stand on 4 plates and top each with an egg. Serve straight away.

Catalan Style Pasta — serves 4

> *350g (12 oz) pasta shells*
> *4 large garlic cloves, crushed*
> *2 level tablespoons tubed or canned tomato concentrate*

2 tablespoons olive oil
salt and pepper to taste
4 hard boiled eggs, chopped or coarsely grated

1.   Cook the pasta in boiling salted water for 8 to 10 minutes or until shells are *just* tender. *Do not* overcook. A little oil added to the cooking water helps to keep the pasta separate and non-sticky.
2.   Drain the pasta thoroughly. Tip into a large dish. Keep hot.
3.   Heat the garlic with the tomato concentrate and oil, allowing about 4 to 5 minutes and stirring continuously. Season.
4.   Add to the pasta and toss thoroughly. Pile onto 4 warm plates and sprinkle with eggs. Serve straight away.

Egg and Avocado 'Mayonnaise' — serves 6

1 standard (size 3) egg
2 tablespoons salad oil
2 tablespoons cider vinegar
1 packet (about 75g or 3 oz) Philadelphia cream cheese
1 medium avocado
1 level teaspoon prepared mild mustard
½ to 1 level teaspoon salt
3 to 4 tablespoons boiling water
6 large hard boiled eggs

Garnish
mustard and cress
grated carrot

1.   To make the 'mayonnaise', place the egg, oil, vinegar and cream cheese into blender goblet. Blend until smooth.
2.   Peel the avocado as you would peel a pear, starting from the pointed end. Cut directly into the blender. Re-blend until very smooth, wiping down sides of blender whenever necessary.
3.   Spoon into a bowl. Beat in the mustard and salt, and sufficient boiling water to make the 'mayonnaise' of coating consistency.
4.   Slice the eggs into a shallow dish. Spread the avocado mixture over the top. Garnish by sprinkling with mustard and cress. Top prettily with mounds of grated carrot. Serve with brown toast or freshly boiled baby new potatoes, tossed in butter and mint leaves.

Celeriac and Avocado 'Mayonnaise' — serves 6

Make exactly as above, substituting ¾kg (1½ lb) cooked and sliced celeriac for the eggs. The celeriac must be *cold*.

Avocado Mousse — serves 6

> *2 tablespoons lemon juice*
> *1 tablespoon cider vinegar*
> *2 large avocados*
> *2 large garlic cloves, crushed*
> *150ml (¼ pt) soured cream*
> *150g (¼ pt) double cream, softly whipped*
> *2 teaspoons Dijon mustard*
> *1 level teaspoon salt*
> *3 tablespoons milk*
> *3 standard eggs, separated*
> *1 envelope (4 level teaspoons) powdered gelatine*
> *2 tablespoons cold water*

1. Pour the lemon juice and cider vinegar into a blender goblet. Peel the avocados as you would peel a pear, starting from the pointed end. Cut directly into the blender.
2. Add the garlic cloves (already crushed) and the soured cream. Blend until absolutely smooth. Spoon into a bowl.
3. Fold in the cream, mustard, salt, milk and egg yolks. When smooth and evenly combined, leave on one side temporarily.
4. Soften the gelatine for 5 minutes in the cold water. (Do this in a saucepan.) Stand the pan over a low heat. Leave until the gelatine dissolves, but do not allow to boil.
5. In a clean and dry bowl, beat the egg whites to a stiff and airy snow. Fold into the avocado mixture alternately with the gelatine. Work slowly and gently, ensuring that the texture is completely smooth, light and consistent in colour; there should be no streakiness.
6. Chill until just *beginning* to thicken and set. Spoon into 6 glass dishes. Refrigerate until completely set. Serve unadorned or garnish to taste with Spanish sliced stuffed olives, watercress, chopped parsley etc.

Eggs Flamenco — serves 4

> *4 medium tomatoes, blanched and skinned*
> *8 Spanish stuffed olives*
> *2 canned red peppers (pimentos)*
> *125g (4 oz) button mushrooms*
> *salt and pepper*
> *4 large eggs*
> *25g (1 oz) butter, melted*

1. Slice the tomatoes and olives. Cut the peppers into thin strips. Break each mushroom into halves or quarters, depending on size. Mix these 4 ingredients well together. Season with salt and pepper.

2.   Divide the mixture equally over the base of 4 well-buttered ovenproof dishes. Each should measure no less than 10cm (4 in) in diameter. Bake near the top of moderately hot oven (200°C/400°F, Gas 6) for 10 minutes.
3.   Remove from the oven. Break an egg into each over the vegetables. Coat with melted butter. Bake for a further 5 to 6 minutes or until eggs are only *just* set.
4.   Serve straight away. Accompany with boiled new potatoes tossed in butter, or well-creamed potatoes flavoured with a touch of grated nutmeg.

Spanish Style Tortilla with Olives — serves 4

> *3 tablespoons olive oil*
> *225g (8 oz) onion, finely chopped or grated*
> *½kg (1 lb) potatoes, par-boiled and diced*
> *75g (3 oz) Spanish stuffed olives, sliced*
> *6 standard (size 3) eggs*
> *1 level teaspoon salt*
> *freshly milled pepper to taste*

1.   Heat the oil in a large and heavy-based frying pan measuring about 25cm (10 in) in diameter. If the pan is non-stick, so much the better.
2.   Add the onion and potato dice. Fry over a moderate heat until both are golden, turning from time to time. This should take between 10 and 15 minutes. Stir in the olives.
3.   Beat the eggs thoroughly with salt and pepper to taste. Pour into the pan over the vegetables. Cook over a moderate heat until set and browned underneath.
4.   To turn over, place a *large* plate on top of the frying pan then tip the pan upside down. The omelet or Tortilla should fall onto the plate. Carefully slide back into the pan — browned side up — and cook for a further 2 to 3 minutes to brown the underside.
5.   Again turn out on to a large, warm plate and cut into 4 portions. Serve with grilled tomatoes.

Macaroni in Blue Cheese Cream Sauce — serves 4

> *125g (4 oz) whole wheat short cut macaroni*
> *125g (4 oz) short cut macaroni*
> *575ml (1 pt) water*
> *1 level teaspoon salt*
> *1 teaspoon salad oil*
> *150ml (¼ pt) double cream*
> *2 standard eggs*
> *175g (6 oz) blue cheese, crumbled*

salt and freshly milled pepper to taste
paprika for sprinkling over top

1. Cook the macaroni (both varieties together) in water with salt and oil for about 10 minutes. Do not overcook or the pasta will become bloated and soggy.
2. Drain thoroughly and return to the saucepan. Stand over a minimal heat. Beat the cream and eggs well together. Add to the macaroni with the crumbled blue cheese and seasoning.
3. Toss over and over with 2 spoons until the pasta is piping hot and the eggs look as though they are lightly scrambled.
4. Pile onto 4 warm plates and sprinkle each with paprika. Serve with a crisp salad.

Belgian Chicory 'Braise' — serves 4

3 tablespoons salad oil
225g (8 oz) onions, chopped
6 medium heads Belgian chicory, washed
½kg (1 lb) peeled potatoes, diced
1 level teaspoon salt
4 tablespoons water

To Serve
4 freshly fried eggs

1. Heat the oil in a heavy-based pan. Add the onion. Fry gently for about 10 minutes or until pale gold.
2. Meanwhile, remove the 'cores' from the base of each chicory head (this part is very bitter and best discarded). With a stainless knife, cut the chicory into shreds.
3. Add to the pan of onions. Continue to fry a further 5 to 7 minutes or until light gold. Add the last 3 ingredients.
4. Cover the pan. Simmer for 12 to 15 minutes or until the potatoes are tender. Pile onto 4 warm plates and top each with a fried egg.

Eggs Chasseur — serves 4

25g (1 oz) butter
2 teaspoons salad oil
1 small onion, finely chopped
6 medium cup mushrooms, finely chopped
2 level tablespoons flour
275ml (½ pt) dry red wine
4 level tablespoons tubed or canned tomato concentrate

1 level teaspoon caster sugar
1 level teaspoon Dijon mustard
2 tablespoons brandy
1 level tablespoon chopped parsley
8 freshly poached eggs
4 slices hot buttered toast

1.   Heat the butter and oil in a heavy-based frying pan. Add onions and mushrooms. Fry gently for about 15 minutes or until the vegetables are soft and the onions just beginning to brown. It may take a few minutes longer, depending on the liquid content of the onions and mushrooms.
2.   Stir in the flour and cook for 2 minutes. Gradually blend in the wine. Cook, stirring non-stop, until the sauce comes to the boil and thickens. Whisk in the next 5 ingredients.
3.   Simmer the sauce for about 5 minutes, stirring frequently. Transfer the eggs to the toast (two on each slice). Stand on warm plates then coat generously with the sauce. Serve straight away.

Avocado Lettuce Crown with Tomatoes — serves 4

2 lettuce hearts
2 medium avocados
1 tablespoon lemon juice
½ level teaspoon salt
1 rounded tablespoon bottled sauce tartare
2 medium garlic cloves, crushed
½kg (1 lb) blanched tomatoes, skinned and chopped

1.   Cut each lettuce heart into 4 pieces. Arrange the 8 pieces in a ring on a large plate.
2.   Halve the avocados, remove the stones and scoop the flesh into a bowl. Mash finely with lemon juice.
3.   Season to taste with salt then stir in the sauce tartare and garlic cloves. Spoon over the lettuce. Finally top with the chopped tomatoes.
4.   Serve straight away with crispbreads and butter.

Tomato Tart Lyonnaise — serves 4

Shortcrust pastry made with 175g (6 oz) plain flour

Filling
175g (6 oz) tomatoes
75g (3 oz) onions
25g (1 oz) butter

275ml (½ pt) milk
3 standard eggs
salt and pepper to taste
25g (1 oz) grated Parmesan cheese

1.   Set the oven to moderately hot, 200°C/400°F, Gas 6. Well grease a 20cm (8 in) fluted flan dish or a fluted flan ring standing on a buttered baking tray.
2.   Line the base and sides with pastry, first rolled out on a floured surface. Leave in refrigerator temporarily.
3.   Blanch and skin the tomatoes. Chop. Chop or grate the peeled onions. Heat the butter in a pan. When hot and bubbly, add the onions and fry gently, uncovered, until pale gold. Stir in the tomatoes. Continue to cook, stirring from time to time, until the mixture is thick. This will take about ¼ hour and the heat under the pan should be medium. Stand aside for the moment.
4.   Beat the milk and eggs well together. Season to taste with salt and pepper. Cover the base of the tart with the tomato and onion mixture. Carefully pour in the beaten milk and eggs. Sprinkle with Parmesan cheese.
5.   Stand just above the centre of the oven. Reduce the temperature straightaway to 180°C/350°F, Gas 4. Continue to bake for about ¾ hour when the filling should be set like a baked custard and the pastry pale gold and biscuity-looking.
6.   Remove from the oven and serve hot or cold, cut into healthy-sized wedges. Accompany with salad to taste.

Creamy Noodle and Spinach Layer — serves 4

225g (8 oz) flat ribbon noodles
boiling salted water
1 can (about 275g/10 oz) spinach purée
50g (2 oz) walnuts, finely ground
1 carton (150ml/¼ pt) soured cream
1 or 2 large pinches grated nutmeg
275ml (½ pt) freshly made white sauce
175g (6 oz) Cheddar cheese, finely grated
1 level teaspoon prepared mustard
salt and pepper to taste
25g (1 oz) butter

1.   Cook the noodles in boiling water for about 7 to 10 minutes or until just tender. *Do not* overcook or the pasta will become bloated and soggy.
2.   Drain thoroughly. Use half to line the base of a well-buttered and shallow oblong heatproof dish.

3.   Combine the spinach with the walnuts, soured cream and nutmeg. If necessary, season to taste with salt and pepper. Spread over the noodles in the dish. Top with the rest of the noodles.

4.   Stand the sauce over a low heat. Add two-thirds of the cheese, mustard and salt and pepper to taste. Pour over the noodles in the dish. Sprinkle with the rest of the cheese.

5.   Dot with flakes of butter. Reheat and brown for 20 to 25 minutes in a hot oven set to 220°C/425°F, Gas 7. Serve with fried tomato halves.

Dutch Broad Bean, Pepper and Tomato Casserole — serves 6

> *¾kg (1½ lb) broad beans (shelled weight)*
> *boiling salted water*
> *50g (2 oz) butter*
> *2 teaspoons salad oil*
> *125g (4 oz) onion, chopped*
> *1 medium green pepper, de-seeded and cut into thin strips*
> *1 medium red pepper, de-seeded and cut into thin strips*
> *225g (8 oz) blanched tomatoes, skinned and chopped*
> *4 large slices white or brown bread*
> *75g (3 oz) extra butter*
> *3 teaspoons salad oil*

1.   Cook the beans in the boiling salted water for about 15 minutes or until just tender. Drain. Leave on one side temporarily.

2.   Heat the butter and oil in a sturdy frying pan. Add the onion. Fry for about 20 minutes or until pale gold. Keep the heat moderate under the pan. Add the peppers and tomatoes. Fry for a further 10 minutes, turning frequently.

3.   Stir in the drained beans. Cover the pan. Heat through for 10 minutes. Meanwhile, cut the bread into small dice. Fry in the butter and oil until crisp and golden-brown.

4.   Transfer the vegetable mixture to a warm dish and sprinkle with fried bread cubes. Serve with freshly poached eggs.

Gratin Dauphinoise — serves 8

> *1½kg (3 lb) old potatoes*
> *1 large garlic clove*
> *75g (3 oz) butter, melted*
> *1½ level teaspoons salt*
> *white pepper to taste*
> *175g (6 oz) Gruyère cheese*
> *275ml (½ pt) single cream*

1. Peel the potatoes and cut into wafer-thin slices; I usually achieve the best results when I 'shred' the potatoes on a hand-held grater. Stand in a bowl of water and leave for about 1 hour to remove as much starch as possible. Drain. Dry off in a teatowel.

2. Press the cut garlic clove against the base and sides of a heatproof dish measuring about 30cm (12 in) square by 2½cm (1 in) in depth. Brush heavily with melted butter.

3. Cover the base of the dish with half the potatoes. Trickle half the butter on top, season to taste with salt and pepper then sprinkle with half the cheese.

4. Cover with the rest of the potatoes. Season again. Coat with butter and sprinkle with the rest of the cheese.

5. Bring the cream just up to the boil. Pour slowly down the side of the dish. Cook for 30 minutes in a hot oven set to 220°C/400°F, Gas 7. If the potatoes are still on the hard side, return to the oven for a further 5 to 10 minutes. Serve with salad.

Pissaladiere (French Onion Tart) — serves about 6

> *175g (6 oz) shortcrust pastry made from 175g (6 oz) plain flour*
> *1kg (2 lb) onions, very thinly sliced*
> *3 garlic cloves, crushed*
> *4 tablespoons olive oil*
> *½ level teaspoon mixed herbs*
> *1 small bay leaf*
> *salt and pepper to taste*

> **Topping**
> *20 to 24 small black olives*
> *1 extra tablespoon olive oil*
> *salt, freshly milled pepper, nutmeg*

1. Roll out the pastry. Use to line a 20cm (8 in) flan ring standing on a buttered baking tray. Line the base and sides with foil to prevent the pastry from rising as it bakes. Refrigerate until ready for use.

2. Place all the remaining ingredients in a heavy pan. Cook *very slowly* for ¾ hour. Keep the pan covered. Uncover. If there is a gathering of excess liquid — bearing in mind the onions should be as thick as a purée — cook, uncovered, for a further 20 to 40 minutes. Stir frequently to prevent burning.

3. Remove the bay leaf. Leave the onion mixture on one side temporarily. Bake the pastry case for ¼ hour in a hot oven set to 220°C/425°F, Gas 7. Remove the foil carefully.

4. Fill the cooked pastry case with the prepared onion mixture then stud

with the olives. Trickle the olive oil over the top. Sprinkle with salt, freshly milled pepper and a whisper of nutmeg. Bake for 15 to 20 minutes in an oven set to 200°C/400°F, Gas 6, when the filling should be piping hot and bubbling and the surrounding pastry golden-brown. Cut into wedges to serve.

Crusty Bread and Butter Pudding with Mushrooms — serves 4

4 large slices white bread, de-crusted
50g (2 oz) butter
125g (4 oz) mild Cheddar cheese, grated
2 level tablespoons finely chopped parsley
1 small onion, finely grated
salt and pepper to taste
150ml (¼ pt) single cream
2 standard (size 3) eggs, beaten with 1 extra yolk
225g (8 oz) sliced and butter-fried mushrooms

1.   Spread the bread fairly thickly with butter. Cut each slice into 4 fingers. Arrange half the fingers over the base of a 1¼l (2 pt) buttered dish.
2.   Sprinkle the bread with three-quarters of the cheese, the parsley, onion and salt and pepper to taste.
3.   Place the rest of the bread fingers, buttered sides uppermost, on top.
4.   Whisk the cream and eggs well together. Pour gently into the dish over the bread.
5.   Sprinkle with the remaining cheese and leave to stand for ½ hour. Bake for about 40/45 minutes in a moderately hot oven set to 190°C/375°F, Gas 5, when the pudding should be well puffed and deep gold.
6.   Smother with freshly fried mushrooms and serve while still very hot. Baked tomatoes make an excellent accompaniment.

Bulgarian Guvetch — serves 6

½kg (1 lb) onions, chopped
6 tablespoons salad oil (in Bulgaria they would probably use sunflower oil)
4 to 6 garlic cloves, finely chopped
1kg (2 lb) green and red peppers, mixed in equal quantities
½kg (1 lb) French beans
¾kg (1½ lb) blanched tomatoes, chopped
4 tablespoons tubed or canned tomato concentrate
1 fresh chilli (very hot, so beware!)
2 level teaspoons salt

1.   In large and heavy-based saucepan, fry the onions in the oil very slowly until pale gold. Keep the pan covered and allow about 30 minutes, when onions should be soft.

2.   Add the garlic and stir in well. De-seed peppers and cut the flesh into strips. Top and tail the beans and remove the side strings if necessary. Snap each into 3 or 4 pieces. Add the pepper strips and beans to the pan with all the remaining ingredients.

3.   Stir well to mix. Bring slowly to the boil, stirring. Cover. Cook for 1 to 1¼ hours or until the vegetables are very soft. Uncover. Continue to cook over low heat until the vegetable mixture thickens to a stew-like consistency and very little liquid remains. Remove chilli.

4.   Serve hot with rice or pasta. Alternately, cool Guvetch completely. Chill in the refrigerator for several hours. Serve as a topping on cold boiled potatoes and accompany with hard boiled eggs and squares of goat's milk cheese.

Cheese and Tarragon Loaf — serves about 6

> ½kg (1 lb) self raising flour
> 2 level teaspoons salt
> 2 level teaspoons dry mustard
> 25g (1 oz) butter
> 125g (4 oz) Edam cheese, finely grated
> 1 level teaspoon dried tarragon
> 275ml (½ pt) milk
> a little egg for brushing

1.   Sift the flour, salt and mustard into bowl. Rub in the butter. Add the cheese and tarragon.

2.   Mix to a soft dough with the milk. Turn on to floured surface. Knead lightly until smooth. Shape into a 25cm (10 in) loaf, tapering the ends.

3.   Place on greased tray and brush the top with egg. Bake for about 50 minutes to 1 hour in moderately hot oven set to 200°C/400°F, Gas 6.

4.   The loaf is ready when it is well risen and brown and also when a skewer, pushed gently into the centre, come out clean without uncooked pieces of mixture clinging to it. Cool on a wire rack, slice and butter when cold. Serve with whole tomatoes, sliced cucumber and clusters of watercress.

Romanian Polenta with Cheese — serves 4

> ¾l (1¼ pt) cold water
> 150g (5 oz) yellow polenta (coarse corn meal) or coarse semolina
> 3 level teaspoons salt
> 125g (4 oz) butter
> 175g (6 oz) mild Cheddar cheese, finely grated
> 1 standard (size 3) egg
> 150ml (¼ pt) double cream
> salt and pepper to taste

1. Set oven to moderately hot 200°C/400°F, Gas 6. Well butter a 1¼l (2 pt) casserole.
2. Pour the water into a pan. Add the polenta or coarse semolina and salt. Bring to the boil, stirring continuously. Cook for about 5 minutes over a medium heat when the mixture should be very thick.
3. Stir in half the butter. Cover the base of a prepared casserole with half the polenta. Sprinkle with two-thirds of the cheese.
4. Dot with the rest of the butter. Spread the remaining polenta or semolina mixture smoothly over the top.
5. Sprinkle with the left-over cheese. Beat the egg and cream well together. Pour into the casserole over the cheese. Sprinkle with salt and pepper.
6. Bake for 30/40 minutes or until the polenta mixture is piping hot and bubbly on top. Serve straight away with a salad to taste.
Note
To make this a more substantial meal, top each portion of Polenta with a freshly poached egg.

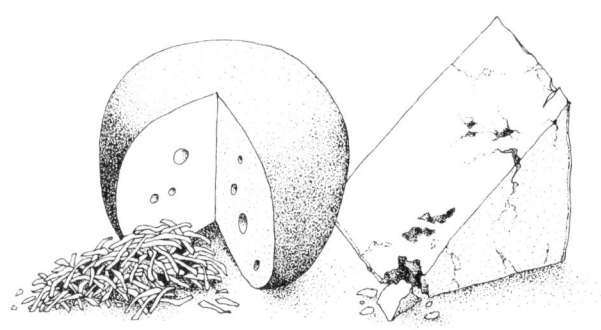

Dropped Raisin Scones — serves 4

> *225g (8 oz) self raising flour*
> *½ level teaspoon dry mustard*
> *½ level teaspoon salt*
> *50g (2 oz) mature Cheddar cheese, very finely grated*
> *50g (2 oz) seedless raisins*
> *1 standard (grade 3) egg*
> *275ml (½ pt) milk*
> *50g (2 oz) butter, melted*

1. Sift the flour, mustard and salt into bowl. Add the cheese and raisins.
2. Mix to a smooth and creamy batter with a whole egg and half the milk. Whisk until smooth.

3.   Stir in the rest of the milk with the butter. Refrigerate 30 minutes.
4.   Brush a large pan (preferably non-stick) with melted butter or oil and heat until hot. Drop small rounds of the scone mixture — about 12 in total — from a spoon into the pan. (You will probably manage 4/6 at a time, depending on size of pan.)
5.   Cook until bubbles appear on the top and burst; this should take about 2/3 minutes over a medium heat.
6.   Carefully turn over with a knife or spatula and cook for a further 1 to 1½ minutes.
7.   Pile the scones in a clean and folded teatowel to keep warm. Serve with extra butter for spreading, as well as lightly boiled eggs and a salad to taste.

Dropped Scones with Cheese and Parsley — serves 4

If preferred, the raisins may be omitted and a heaped tablespoon of chopped parsley used in their place.

Pancakes Neapolitan — serves 4

> *1 can (about 400g/14 oz) tomatoes*
> *1 small onion, grated*
> *1 level teaspoon salt*
> *1 level teaspoon basil*
> *1 teaspoon lemon juice*
> *8 already cooked pancakes*
> *75g (3 oz) grated Parmesan cheese*
> *75g (3 oz) Cheddar cheese, grated*
> *1 level tablespoon lightly toasted breadcrumbs*

1.   Turn the tomatoes into a 25cm (10 in) shallow, square casserole dish. Mash the tomatoes with a fork to break them up. Stir in the onion, salt, basil and lemon juice. Slowly bring to boil, stirring.
2.   Fold the pancakes first in half and then in half again. Add to the tomato mixture. Cover. Simmer gently for 10 minutes.
3.   Uncover. Sprinkle with both the cheeses and the breadcrumbs. Brown under a hot grill and serve with freshly cooked leaf spinach.

Main Course Dinner Dishes

Poached Eggs Pizzaiola — serves 6

¾kg (1½ lb) tomatoes, blanched and skinned
25g (1 oz) butter
2 tablespoons olive oil
3 large garlic cloves, finely chopped or crushed
2 level teaspoons salt
½ level teaspoon each oregano and basil
2 tablespoons tubed or canned tomato concentrate
5 tablespoons water
1 level teaspoon caster sugar
grated Parmesan cheese

To serve
6 slices de-crusted white or brown bread, freshly fried in butter with a dash of oil
6 freshly poached eggs

1. Put the tomatoes into a heavy-based pan with the next 4 ingredients. Simmer, uncovered, until most of the liquid has cooked away and you are left with a thickish tomato 'stew'.

2. Stir in the herbs, tomato concentrate, water and sugar. Bring to the boil, stirring. Simmer for 10 minutes with the lid on the pan.
3. To serve, place the bread on 6 individual warm plates. Top with the eggs. Coat with tomato sauce and sprinkle with cheese. Serve straight away.

Spaghetti Pizzaiola — serves 6

Make a tomato sauce exactly as directed above, but instead of serving it with eggs on fried bread, spoon it over any freshly boiled pasta to taste, allowing about 75g (3 oz) raw weight per person. Sprinkle with grated Parmesan cheese mixed with grated lemon peel (about 1 level teaspoon) and chopped parsley to taste.

Egg, Cheese and Onion Pasties — serves 6

> *3 hard boiled eggs*
> *175g (6 oz) sage Derby cheese, grated (or use Cheddar)*
> *1 small onion, grated*
> *1 level tablespoon chopped parsley*
> *1 level tablespoon chopped chives*
> *2 level tablespoons chutney*
> *1 standard (grade 3) egg, beaten*
> *salt and pepper to taste*
> *shortcrust pastry made with 350g (12 oz) plain flour*
> *beaten egg for brushing*

1. Chop the eggs and place in a bowl. Mix with the cheese, onion, parsley and chives. Stir in the chutney. Bind with the beaten egg. Season to taste with salt and pepper.
2. Roll out the pastry into a rectangle measuring 45cm by 30cm (18 in by 12 in). Trim edges to neaten. Cut the rectangle into 6 by 15cm (6 in) squares.
3. Spread the filling over each square to within 2½cm (1 in) of the edges. Dampen the edges with water. Fold over to form triangles. Pinch the edges well together to seal.
4. Transfer to a large buttered baking tray. Brush with egg. Bake in a hot oven set to 220°C/400°F, Gas 6, allowing 20 to 30 minutes when pasties should be golden brown. Serve hot or cold with salad.

Cottage Cheese Pasties — serves 6

If preferred make a filling from the following: 350g (12 oz) cottage cheese mixed with 2 tablespoons chutney, 25g (1 oz) chopped salted peanuts, 1 level teaspoon finely grated onion, 2 tablespoons yogurt and salt and pepper to taste.

Three-Nut Burgers — serves 4

125g (4 oz) ground almonds
125g (4 oz) walnuts, ground
125g (4 oz) Brazil nuts, ground
crumbs from 4 large slices brown bread
125g (4 oz) onion, grated
1 garlic clove, crushed
1 level teaspoon salt
1 level teaspoon dry mustard
2 standard (grade 3) eggs
oil for frying

Garnish
8 lemon wedges
1 level tablespoon drained capers, chopped

1.   Place all the ingredients, except the oil, into a mixing bowl. Using a fork, mix to a fairly stiff paste.
2.   Shape into 8 cakes with damp hands, making them as even as possible.
3.   Fry in hot oil until golden on both sides. Allow about 4 to 5 minutes and turn twice.
4.   Garnish the burgers with lemon wedges and capers. Serve hot with sauté potatoes and green vegetables to taste.

Peanut Burgers — serves 4

350g (12 oz) salted peanuts, ground
1 level teaspoon curry powder
1 level teaspoon finely grated lemon peel
1 level teaspoon paprika
1 small onion, grated
½ level teaspoon salt
crumbs from 4 large slices white bread
2 standard (grade 3) eggs, beaten
2 tablespoons milk
oil for frying

Garnish
8 freshly grilled button mushrooms
sprigs of watercress

1.   Place all the ingredients, except the oil, into mixing bowl. Using a fork, mix to a fairly stiff paste.
2.   Shape into 8 cakes with damp hands, making them as neat as possible.

3. Fry in hot oil until golden on both sides, allowing about 5 minutes and turning twice.

4. Garnish with mushrooms and watercress. Serve with baked jacket potatoes and mixed salad.

Mushroom Pizza Neapolitan — serves 3 to 4

225g (8 oz) white bread dough (uncooked and allowed to rise once)

Topping
150g (5 oz) tubed or canned tomato concentrate
1 large garlic clove, crushed
2 tablespoons olive oil
1 level teaspoon caster sugar
1 level teaspoon salt
350g (12 oz) blanched tomatoes, skinned and sliced
2 level teaspoons chopped parsley
1 level teaspoon basil
225g (8 oz) Mozzarella cheese
125g (4 oz) trimmed mushrooms, sliced
16 black olives
2 extra tablespoons olive oil

1. Roll out the bread dough thinly. Use to cover an oiled Pizza tin measuring 30cm (12 in) in diameter. (In the absence of a round tin, use a large Swiss roll one measuring 32½cm by 22½cm (13 by 9 in).) Leave to rise in a warm place for about 20 minutes.

2. Meanwhile heat together the tomato concentrate, garlic, oil, sugar and salt. Stir over a low heat until well-mixed. Spread over the Pizza base. Top with sliced tomatoes.

3. Sprinkle with parsley and basil. Cover with slices of cheese topped with mushrooms and olives. Trickle the rest of the olive oil over the top. Bake for about 25 to 30 minutes in a moderately hot oven set to 200°C/400°F, Gas 6.

4. Cut into 3 or 4 pieces and eat while still hot.

Eggs à la King — serves 6

1 small red pepper
125g (4 oz) mushrooms
25g (1 oz) butter
275ml (½ pt) freshly made white sauce
12 hard boiled eggs, sliced
150ml (¼ pt) single cream

2 egg yolks
1 tablespoon lemon juice
pinch of grated nutmeg
½ level teaspoon prepared American mustard
salt and pepper to taste

1.   Wash and dry the pepper. Halve. Remove the inside fibres and seeds and discard. Cut the flesh into thin strips. Trim the mushrooms. Wash if necessary then dry. Slice.
2.   Heat the butter in a saucepan. As soon as it begins to sizzle, add the pepper and mushrooms. Cover the pan and fry gently for 7 minutes.
3.   Stir into the white sauce (include any remaining butter and juices) with the eggs. Heat through for 3 minutes. Take off heat.
4.   Beat together the next 5 ingredients. Stir into the sauce mixture. Season well to taste. Reheat for about 3 minutes, stirring all the time.
5.   Serve with freshly boiled rice or atop freshly made brown toast. Corn Fritters (see recipe below) are also excellent with the Eggs à la King.

Corn Fritters — makes 16

125g (4 oz) self raising flour
½ level teaspoon salt
½ level teaspoon dry mustard
1 standard egg
275ml (½ pt) cold milk
4 rounded tablespoons canned sweetcorn, drained
melted butter or salad oil for frying

1.   Sift the flour, salt and mustard into a bowl. Beat to a smooth and creamy batter with the egg and milk. Stir in the sweetcorn.
2.   Brush a sturdy frying pan with melted butter or oil. Heat until hot. Drop small rounds of the mixture, a few at a time, into the frying pan.
3.   Cook until the undersides are golden. Turn over when bubbles rise to the surface and break. Fry for a further 1 to 2 minutes. Serve warm.

Florence Fennel in Cheesey Pernod Sauce — serves 4

¾kg (1½ lb) Florence fennel, trimmed
cold water
juice of 1 medium lemon
1½ level teaspoons salt
40g (1½ oz) butter
40g (1½ oz) flour
275ml (½ pt) water in which fennel was cooked
150ml (¼ pt) single cream

175g (6 oz) red Cheshire cheese
1 level teaspoon French mustard
1 tablespoon Pernod
salt and pepper to taste

Topping
4 tablespoons double cream
25g (1 oz) butter

1.   Put the fennel into a large pan. Cover with water. Add the lemon juice (which helps to keep fennel a good colour) and salt. Bring to the boil.
2.   Simmer for about 30 to 40 minutes or until the fennel is just tender. Drain and slice. Reserve 275ml (½ pt) of the cooking water from the fennel.
3.   Melt the butter in a clean pan. Stir in the flour. Cook for 2 minutes, stirring all the time to prevent browning. Gradually blend in the fennel water and cream.
4.   Cook, stirring all the time, until the sauce comes to boil and thickens. Add two-thirds of the cheese with the mustard and Pernod. Season. Replace the fennel. Heat through. Turn into a greased heatproof dish.
5.   Sprinkle the rest of the cheese on top, then add dollops of cream and flakes of butter. Brown under a hot grill. Accompany with freshly cooked baby carrots tossed in butter and sprinkled with chopped parsley or fresh dill.

Parsnip Pancakes — serves 4

½kg (1 lb) parsnips, cooked and mashed
125g (4 oz) onion, grated
1 level teaspoon salt
2 standard (size 3) eggs, beaten
50g (2 oz) self raising flour
oil for frying

1.   In a large bowl, combine the parsnips with the onions, salt, eggs and flour. Mix thoroughly. Leave to stand for about 15 minutes.
2.   With damp hands, shape into 12 flattish cakes. Heat about 1¼cm (½ in) of oil in a large and heavy-based frying pan.
3.   Fry the pancakes, about 4 at a time, until crisp and golden brown.
4.   Turn twice and allow a total of 5 to 6 minutes frying time.
5.   Drain thoroughly on paper towels and serve hot with freshly fried eggs and cold apple sauce.

Scolloped Potatoes in Brie Sauce — serves 4

¾kg (1½ lb) potatoes, boiled
1 medium onion, grated

3 level tablespoons finely chopped parsley
salt and pepper to taste
40g (1½ oz) butter
40g (1½ oz) flour
350ml (¾ pt) milk
175g (6 oz) Brie cheese
1 level teaspoon paprika

Topping
2 level tablespoon lightly toasted breadcrumbs
25g (1 oz) butter

1.   Slice the potatoes fairly thickly. Use half to cover the base of a shallow, buttered heatproof dish. Sprinkle with onion, parsley and salt and pepper to taste. Cover with the rest of the potato.
2.   To make the sauce, melt the butter in a pan. Stir in the flour and cook for 2 minutes without browning. Gradually blend in the milk. Cook, stirring continuously, until the sauce comes to the boil and thickens. Leave over a minimal heat.
3.   Cut the Brie cheese into thin slivers. Add to the sauce and stir until half melted. Add paprika and season to taste with salt and pepper.
4.   Pour the sauce evenly over the potatoes. Sprinkle with crumbs and dot with flakes of butter. Reheat and brown for 15 to 20 minutes in a hot oven set to 220°C/425°F, Gas 7. Serve very hot with butter fried mushrooms and fried tomato halves.

Balkan Creamed Egg and Potato Bake — serves 6

125g (4 oz) onion, chopped
50g (2 oz) butter
2 teaspoons salad oil
1kg (2 lb) freshly boiled potatoes
8 hard boiled eggs
salt and pepper to taste
275ml (½ pt) double cream

1.   Set the oven to moderately hot, 200°C/400°F, Gas 6. Well butter a medium-sized roasting tin.
2.   In large and heavy-based pan, fry the onion slowly in the butter and oil until very pale gold.
3.   Dice the potatoes and add to the pan of onions. Spoon the mix gently together.
4.   Use to cover the base of a buttered tin.
5.   Coarsely chop the eggs and sprinkle over the potatoes. Season to taste with salt and pepper then spoon the cream evenly over the top.

6.   Reheat for about 25 minutes. Serve with green vegetables to taste or a mixed salad.

Cheesey Macaroni and Tomato Hot Pot — serves 6

> *225g (8 oz) short cut macaroni*
> *40g (1½ oz) butter*
> *40g (1½ oz) flour*
> *575ml (1 pt) milk*
> *175g (6 oz) mild Cheddar cheese, grated*
> *2 level tablespoons tubed or canned tomato concentrate*
> *1 small onion, grated*
> *1 level teaspoon salt*
> *1 level teaspoon prepared mustard*
> *white pepper to taste*

1.   Cook the macaroni as directed on the packet, allowing about 8 to 10 minutes. Drain.
2.   Set the oven to moderately hot, 190°C/375°F, Gas 5. Well-butter a 1½l (2½ pt) heatproof dish.
3.   Melt the butter in saucepan. Stir in the flour. Gradually blend in the milk.
4.   Cook, stirring continuously, until the sauce comes to the boil and thickens.
5.   Add 125g (4 oz) cheese to the sauce with the drained macaroni, tomato concentrate, grated onion and seasonings. Mix thoroughly.
6.   Transfer to a buttered dish then sprinkle the remaining cheese on top. Re-heat and brown near the top of the oven for about 20/30 minutes.
7.   Serve with either green vegetables to taste or a mixed salad.

Tropical Eggs — serves 6

> *70g (2 oz) butter*
> *125g (4 oz) onion, finely chopped*
> *225g (8 oz) American long grain rice*
> *4 large canned pineapple rings, cut into small wedges*
> *575ml (1 pt) boiling water*
> *2 level teaspoons salt*

> **Topping**
> *12 standard eggs*
> *150ml (¼ pt) single cream*
> *2 level teaspoons salt*
> *pepper to taste*
> *4 medium bananas*

1 level tablespoon soft brown sugar
1 level tablespoon desiccated coconut
40g (1½ oz) butter

1.   Heat the butter in a heavy-based pan. When hot and sizzling, add the onion and fry gently until pale gold.
2.   Stir in the rice and pineapple. Fry for 2 to 3 minutes, stirring. Add water and salt.
3.   Bring to the boil and lower heat. Stir once or twice with a fork. Cover. Cook for about 15/20 minutes or until the rice grains are tender and fluffy and no liquid remains.
4.   About 5 minutes before the rice is ready, beat the eggs with the cream, add salt and pepper to taste. Scramble lightly in a clean pan.
5.   Spread the pineapple rice over the base of a large, buttered casserole (not too deep). Cover the centre with scrambled egg.
6.   Peel the bananas then split each in half lengthwise. Stand on top of the eggs.
7.   Sprinkle with sugar and coconut. Add flakes of butter. Brown under a hot grill for 5 minutes. Serve with Brussels sprouts or cauliflower.

Baked Aubergines with Walnuts and Eggs — serves 4

2 large aubergines, washed and dried
boiling salted water
about 2 teaspoons lemon juice
75g (3 oz) butter
175g (6 oz) onion, finely chopped
fresh crumbs from 1 large slice white bread
50g (2 oz) walnuts, finely chopped
3 hard boiled eggs, finely chopped or grated
1 large garlic clove, crushed
3 tablespoons single cream
2 level teaspoons salt
1 tablespoon wine vinegar

1.   Halve the aubergines lengthwise. Carefully cut out the centres, leaving 1¼cm (½ in) thick aubergine shells.
2.   Simmer the shells in boiling salted water for 5 minutes only. Drain. Stand on a buttered baking tray.
3.   Place the insides on a chopping board and sprinkle with lemon juice to prevent browning. Chop finely.
4.   Melt 50g (2 oz) butter in a heavy-based pan. When hot and sizzling, add the onion and fry gently until golden. Stir in the chopped aubergine flesh with all the remaining ingredients. Mix thoroughly.
5.   Mound neatly into the aubergine shells and top with flakes of the

remaining butter. Reheat and brown for about 20 to 25 minutes in an oven set to moderately hot, 200°C/400°F, Gas 6. Serve with brown rice and a mixed salad.

Potato Custard Hot Pot — serves 4 to 6

1kg (2 lb) potatoes, washed and dried
350g (12 oz) mixture of Emmental and Gruyère cheese, finely grated
425ml (¾ pt) milk
3 standard eggs
1 garlic clove, crushed
1 level teaspoon salt
2 level tablespoons breadcrumbs
25g (1 oz) butter

1.   Well butter a 1¾l (3 pt) casserole dish which is deep rather than shallow.
2.   Parboil the potatoes. Drain and rinse under cold water. Leave until completely cold. Cut into slices of about ⅝cm (¼ in) thick.
3.   Fill a buttered dish with alternate layers of the potato slices and two-thirds of the cheese. Beat the milk with eggs, garlic and salt. Strain into the dish over the potato mixture.
4.   Sprinkle with breadcrumbs then top with flakes of butter. Bake for ¾ hour in a moderately hot oven set to 190°C/375°F, Gas 5. Serve hot and accompany with French beans or mange tout.

Cannelloni Cheese Roll-Ups — serves 4

8 cannelloni, cooked as directed on the packet

Filling
175g (6 oz) mature Cheddar cheese, grated
crumbs from 2 large slices white bread (fresh and not toasted bread; include crusts)
1 standard (size 3) egg
3 tablespoons single cream
1 level teaspoon dry mustard
salt and pepper to taste

Topping
½kg (1 lb) large tomatoes, skinned
1 level teaspoon dried basil
225g (8 oz) Mozzarella cheese, sliced fairly thinly

1.   Set the oven to hot, 220°C/425°F, Gas 7. Well butter a fairly shallow heatproof dish.

2. Drain the cannelloni. Split each open and spread out on paper towels to absorb surplus moisture.

3. For the filling, combine the Cheddar cheese with the crumbs. Add all the remaining ingredients. Using a fork, mix thoroughly to form a filling that holds together.

4. Place equal amounts on to the cannelloni. Fold over. Place in prepared dish. Cover with tomatoes, first coarsely chopped. Sprinkle with basil. Finally top with slices of Mozarella cheese.

5. Cook near the top of the oven for 20 to 25 minutes or until piping hot and the cheese has completely melted on top. Serve straight away with a green or mixed salad.

Lancashire Rice 'Hot Pot' — serves 4

> *½kg (1 lb) swede, washed and grated*
> *½kg (1 lb) leeks, trimmed and well-washed*
> *225g (8 oz) American long grain rice*
> *1 can (about 575ml/1 pt) tomato juice*
> *2 to 3 level teaspoons salt*
> *pepper to taste*
> *225g (8 oz) Lancashire cheese, crumbled*

> **Garnish**
> *25g (1 oz) walnuts, very finely chopped*
> *1 large tomato, cut into 8 wedges*

1. Place the swede in a largish saucepan. Slice the leeks and add to the pan with the rice, tomato juice and salt. Season to taste with pepper. Bring to the boil, stirring.

2. Lower the heat. Cover the pan. Simmer for about 25 minutes when the rice grains should be plump and tender and have absorbed all the liquid.

3. Spoon into 4 individual heatproof dishes and sprinkle equal amounts of cheese over each. Brown under a hot grill. Dust with walnuts. Top with tomato wedges. Serve straight away.

Stuffed Eggs in Lemon Sauce — serves 4

> *1 tub mustard and cress*
> *8 large hard boiled eggs*
> *50g (2 oz) Gruyère cheese, finely grated*
> *2 tablespoons milk*
> *6 level teaspoons tubed or canned tomato concentrate*
> *salt and pepper to taste*

> **Sauce**
> *150ml (¼ pt) soured cream*

large pinch salt
1 level teaspoon finely grated lemon peel
1 tablespoon lemon juice

Garnish
chopped mint

1.   Cover the bases of 4 medium-sized plates with mustard and cress. Shell and halve the eggs.
2.   Scoop the egg yolks into a bowl. Add the next 3 ingredients. Season to taste with salt and pepper. Mix well to a smooth paste, adding a little milk if the mixture stays on the dry side.
3.   Mound neatly into egg white halves then stand on the prepared plates (4 halves on each), filled sides uppermost.
4.   To make the sauce, beat the soured cream with the salt, lemon peel and lemon juice. Spoon over the eggs. Garnish by sprinkling with mint. Serve with toast.

Dutch Cheese Dip — serves 6

½kg (1 lb) Gouda cheese, grated
150ml (½ pt) single cream
150ml (½ pt) milk
1 level teaspoon German mustard
2 level tablespoons plain flour
white pepper to taste

To Serve
cubes of about 1 in cut from French bread or
freshly boiled baby new potatoes

1.   Place all the ingredients into a heavy pan. Stir over a low heat, stirring continuously, until the mixture comes to the boil and thickens. Leave to bubble for 1 or 2 minutes.
2.   Stand the pan over a spirit stove and eat the cheese mixture by dipping in cubes of bread or potatoes, speared onto forks.
Note
The Dip is best cooked in a Fondue dish or in a heavy oven-to-table flameproof casserole.

Mixed Vegetables and Ginger Curry with Yogurt — serves 4 to 5

3 tablespoons salad oil
225g (8 oz) onions, finely chopped
6 heaped teaspoons Rogan Josh curry powder

1 level tablespoon Garam Masala
225g (8 oz) fresh okra (ladies' fingers), topped, tailed and cut into 2½cm (1 in) pieces
350g (12 oz) courgettes, cut into 1¼cm (½ in) slices
½kg (1 lb) aubergines, diced (do not peel)
1 medium red pepper, de-seeded and cut into strips
1 medium green pepper, de-seeded and cut into strips
25g (1 oz) fresh ginger, peeled and sliced
2 large garlic cloves, finely chopped
1½ level teaspoons salt
275ml (½ pt) water
150g (5 oz) plain yogurt

1. Heat the oil in a large pan. Add the onions. Fry gently until pale gold. Stir in Rogan Josh and Garam Masala. Cook for 3 or 4 minutes over a very low heat.
2. Add all the prepared vegetables, the ginger, garlic, salt and water. Slowly bring to the boil, stirring. Lower the heat. Cover the pan.
3. Simmer gently for 1 to 1¼ hours or until the vegetables are very soft. Remove from the heat and stir in the yogurt.
4. Serve hot with freshly cooked Basmati rice and mango chutney. Accompany with side dishes of salted peanuts, sliced cucumber, sliced tomatoes and chopped onion.

Party Pepperoni Pasta — serves 10 to 12

12 large red peppers
boiling, salted water for boiling peppers
½kg (1 lb) onions
5 tablespoons salad oil
3 large garlic cloves, crushed
3 level teaspoons salt
150g (5 oz) canned or tubed tomato concentrate

1 can (about 400g/14 oz) peeled tomatoes in purée or tomato juice
2 heaped teaspoons finely chopped parsley
about 1kg (2 lb) freshly cooked macaroni or pasta bows

1.   Wash the peppers. Cut off the tops. Remove the inside fibres and seeds. Discard. In 2 large pans, boil the peppers gently for 10 minutes. Drain thoroughly. Cut into strips.
2.   Peel and finely chop the onions. Fry (in a large pan) in salad oil for ¼ hour. Leave the pan uncovered and the heat very low to prevent the onions from burning, although they should take on a pale gold colour.
3.   Drain the peppers again as you will find there is still an accumulation of liquid clinging to them. Add to the pan with all the remaining ingredients except the pasta.
4.   Break up the tomatoes with a wooden spoon. Slowly bring the mixture to the boil. Lower the heat. Cover. Simmer *very* gently for ¾ hour, stirring from time to time as the mixture tends to catch across the base of the pan.
5.   Serve spooned over individual plates of hot pasta, and top each with either grated Parmesan cheese or a knob of butter.
Note
If you are catering for small numbers, the sauce can be deep frozen up to 9 months if the full amount is not required at one sitting. Half quantity can also be made.

Lasagne Nut Layer — serves about 6

175g (6 oz) lasagne leaves (white)
boiling salted water
a few drops of oil

Filling
75g (3 oz) fresh white breadcrumbs
75g (3 oz) walnuts, peanuts, pecan nuts or hazelnuts, finely ground (or use a
*   mixture of nuts to taste)*

225g (8 oz) cottage cheese, sieved
50g (2 oz) Parmesan cheese, grated
1 medium garlic clove, crushed
1 level teaspoon salt
freshly milled pepper to taste
2 standard eggs, beaten
milk to mix if necessary

Sauce Topping
275ml (½ pt) freshly made white sauce
seasoning to taste
50g (2 oz) Parmesan cheese, grated
50g (2 oz) butter

1. Cook the lasagne, a few leaves at a time, in large frying pan containing boiling salted water and oil (the oil prevents the pasta sticking together).
2. Allow about 7 to 10 minutes cooking time then lift the lasagne out of pan with a fish slice and leave to drain on paper towels.
3. To make the filling, mix all the ingredients (except the milk) thoroughly together. If mixture does not hold together adequately because of dryness, work in a little milk.
4. To complete the lasagne, well butter an oblong dish measuring about 30cm by 17½cm (12 by 7 in). Fill with alternate layers of lasagne leaves and crumb/nut mixture, ending with lasagne.
5. Keep the sauce over a low heat. Season well to taste then stir in the cheese. Spread evenly over the lasagne. Dot with butter. Cook for about 40 minutes in a moderately hot oven set to 190°C/375°F, Gas 5. When ready, the lasagne should be golden and bubbly.
6. Cut into portions and serve with salad or green vegetables to taste.

Cheese 'Escalopes' — serves 4

> *8 slices packeted processed cheese*
> *plain flour*
> *3 standard eggs, well beaten*
> *about 125g (4 oz) lightly toasted breadcrumbs*
> *1 level teaspoon dry mustard*
> *10cm (4 in) corn oil for frying*
> **Garnish**
> *8 grilled tomato halves*
> *8 grilled button mushrooms*
> *4 wedges of lemon*
> *sprigs of watercress*

1. Dip each slice of cheese in flour then coat all over with the beaten eggs.

2. Mix together the crumbs and mustard and place on a piece of foil or greaseproof paper. Add the egg-coated cheese slices and cover well with crumbs, making sure there are no thin patches. This is *essential*, otherwise the cheese will melt too quickly during frying.

3. Re-dip the slices once more in egg and crumbs. Leave to stand for ½ hour for the coating to settle and firm-up.

4. Heat the oil until very hot in a large pan. Add the cheese slices, two at a time. Fry for 45 seconds *only*. Remove from the pan. Drain on paper towels.

5. Garnish each 'escalope' with 2 tomato halves, 2 mushrooms, a wedge of lemon and sprig of watercress. Allow 2 slices per person and accompany with sauté potatoes.

South of the Border Eggs — serves 4

> *50g (2 oz) butter*
> *225g (8 oz) onions, chopped*
> *2 garlic cloves, finely chopped*
> *1 medium aubergine, diced*
> *2 medium green peppers, de-seeded and chopped*
> *¾kg (1½ lb) blanched tomatoes, skinned and chopped*
> *6 eggs*
> *salt and pepper to taste*
> *1 level tablespoon chopped parsley*
> *1 level tablespoon chopped chives*

1. Heat the oven to moderately hot, 200°C/400°F, Gas 6. Well butter an oblong, heatproof casserole dish.

2. Melt butter in a large frying pan. Add the onions and garlic. Fry gently until light gold. Add the rest of the prepared vegetables. Cook slowly, uncovered, for about 20 minutes or until little surplus moisture remains.

3. Beat the eggs well and season to taste with salt and pepper. Pour over the vegetable mixture. Bake in the oven until the eggs are set, allowing about 10 to 20 minutes. You will have to keep a watchful eye on the dish as the eggs might set more quickly than you expect.

4. Remove from the oven. Sprinkle with parsley and chives. Serve with baked jacket potatoes and butter.

Chilli Beans and Chick Peas with Lettuce Cream — serves 6

> *3 round lettuces*
> *2½cm (1 in) boiling water*
> *50g (2 oz) butter*
> *2 large garlic cloves, crushed*
> *2 level tablespoons flour*

150ml (¼ pt) single cream
150ml (¼ pt) milk
1 to 1½ level teaspoons salt
white pepper to taste
3 large pinches grated nutmeg

To serve
1 can (about ½kg or 1 lb) chick peas, drained and rinsed
1 can (about ½kg or 1 lb) American red kidney beans, drained and rinsed
40g (1½ oz) butter

1. Wash the lettuces, removing any damaged outer leaves. Put into a saucepan. Add boiling water. Cover. Boil gently for 10 minutes. Drain.
2. Meanwhile, make the sauce. Melt the butter in a separate pan. Add garlic. Fry *very slowly* for about 7 minutes. Stir in the flour. Cook for 1 minute. Gradually blend in the cream and milk.
3. Cook, stirring continuously, until the sauce comes to the boil and thickens. Stir in lettuces, *first* blended to a smooth purée in a blender goblet.
4. Simmer gently for 4 to 5 minutes, stirring non-stop as the mixture sticks very easily. Season to taste with salt, pepper and nutmeg.
5. Heat together the chick peas and kidney beans in the butter. Spoon onto 6 individual warm plates and coat with the lettuce cream. Accompany with fried tomatoes and mushrooms.

Stir-Fried Almond Rice — serves 4 to 6

2 tablespoons corn or groundnut oil
225g (8 oz) onion, finely chopped
½kg (1 lb) freshly boiled rice (cooked weight)
225g (8 oz) canned bamboo shoots, drained and diced
125g (4 oz) blanched and split almonds, toasted
225g (8 oz) trimmed button mushrooms, very thinly sliced
1 tablespoon soy sauce
6 standard eggs, well-beaten
salt and white pepper to taste

1. Heat the oil in a large pan. Add the onion. Cover the pan. Cook very gently for about ¼ hour when the onion should be soft but still white.
2. Stir in the rice and bamboo shoots. Heat until very hot, fork-stirring all the time. Add the almonds and mushrooms. Mix in well. Heat through for 5 minutes. Stir in soy sauce.
3. Beat the eggs until light and frothy. Season to taste with salt and pepper. Add to the rice mixture. Cook fairly briskly, stirring with a fork all the time, until the eggs are well mixed with the rice mixture and lightly set.

4.   Serve straight away with a salad made from bean sprouts and shredded Chinese leaves, tossed with a mild dressing.

Wholemeal Vegetable Pie — serves 4

425ml (¾ pt) freshly made white sauce
175g (6 oz) Samsoe or Jarlsberg cheese, grated
50g (2 oz) butter
1 teaspoon salad oil
225g (8 oz) onions, chopped
225g (8 oz) celery, thinly sliced
225g (8 oz) diced carrots, cooked
225g (8 oz) diced potato, cooked
50g (2 oz) peas, cooked
salt and pepper to taste

Pastry
175g (6 oz) wholemeal flour
75g (3 oz) butter
about 9 to 10 teaspoons cold water to mix
beaten egg for brushing

1.   Stand the pan of white sauce over a low heat. Add two-thirds of the cheese. Stir until melted. Leave on one side temporarily.
2.   In separate pan, heat the butter and oil until hot. Add the onions and celery. Fry gently for about ¼ hour or until pale gold. Keep the heat low to moderate.
3.   Add to the pan of sauce with the rest of the vegetables. Season to taste with salt and pepper. Cool completely. Place in a 1¼l (2 pt) pie dish with a rim.
4.   To make the pastry, sift the flour into a bowl. Rub in the butter finely. Mix to a fairly stiff dough with the water. Turn out onto a floured surface. Knead lightly until smooth.
5.   Roll out the pastry. From it, cut a piece large enough to fit the top of the pie. Dampen the pie dish rim with water. Line with pastry, cut from trimmings. Moisten again. Cover with the pastry lid. Press edges well together to seal.
6.   Pinch the edges into flutes. Brush the pastry with egg. Bake the pie in a moderately hot oven (200°C/400°F, Gas 6) for 25 to 30 minutes.

Rice Stuffed Peppers with Cheese and Walnuts — serves 6

6 large green peppers
225g (8 oz) American long grain rice

575ml (1 pt) boiling water
1 level teaspoon salt
225g (8 oz) mild Cheddar cheese, grated
1 level teaspoon dry mustard
50g (2 oz) walnuts, coarsely chopped
1 standard (grade 3) egg, beaten
425ml (¾ pt) tomato juice
1 extra teaspoon salt
25g (1 oz) butter, melted

1.   Cut the tops off the peppers and reserve. Remove the inside fibres and seeds and discard. Cut a thin sliver off the base of each pepper so that it stands upright without toppling.
2.   Cook the rice in boiling water and salt for 20 minutes, stirring the ingredients round at the beginning. Keep the pan covered and the heat fairly low. When the rice grains have absorbed all the moisture and are separate and fluffy, tip into a mixing bowl.
3.   Leave until lukewarm. Fork in the cheese, mustard, walnuts and beaten egg. Spoon into the peppers, pushing the mixture well down.
4.   Stand upright in a deep pan and replace the tops. Pour the tomato juice into a pan. Add salt and melted butter. Bring to the boil. Lower the heat and cover.
5.   Simmer over a lowish heat for ½ hour. Serve hot with green vegetables to taste or cold with salad. In either case, baste with pan juices.

Portuguese Style Egg and Pea 'Fry' — serves 6

2 tablespoons olive oil
225g (8 oz) onion, finely chopped or grated
150ml (¼ pt) water
2 large garlic cloves, crushed
½kg (1 lb) fresh peas (shelled weight)
3 rounded tablespoons finely chopped parsley
1 level teaspoon dried coriander
large pinch caster sugar
1 to 1½ level teaspoons salt
white pepper to taste
6 standard (grade 3) eggs

1.   Heat the olive oil in a large and heavy-based frying pan. Add the onion. Fry gently until pale gold.
2.   Stir in all the remaining ingredients except the eggs. Bring to the boil, stirring. Cover the pan. Lower the heat. Simmer for 20 to 25 minutes or until the peas are tender.
3.   Uncover. Break the eggs over the peas etc. Cover. Cook for a further 10

minutes or until the eggs are set. Spoon onto warm plates and serve with boiled potatoes.

Swiss Cheese Party Pie — serves 8 to 10

> *225g (8 oz) white bread dough (uncooked and allowed to rise once)*

Filling
25g (1 oz) butter
2 teaspoons olive oil
175g (6 oz) onions, grated
½kg (1 lb) freshly boiled potatoes (still hot)
½kg (1 lb) Emmental or Gruyère cheese, grated
4 standard (grade 3) eggs, beaten
150ml (¼ pt) single cream
1 level teaspoon salt
white pepper to tase

1. Roll out the dough thinly and use to cover an oiled Pizza tin measuring 30cm (12 in) in diameter. Leave in a warm place to rise while preparing the filling.
2. Heat the butter and oil in a pan. Add the onions. Fry gently until pale gold. Mash the potatoes finely. Spoon into a bowl. Add the fried onions plus the butter and oil in which they were cooked.
3. Work in the rest of the ingredients, beating well to mix. Spread over the dough base to within 2½cm (1 in) of the edges. You will find the filling is fairly thick.
4. Bake for 35 to 40 minutes in a hot oven set to 220°C/400°F, Gas 6. Cut into wedges and serve hot with a crunchy salad.

Turkish Pilav — serves 4 to 6

> *350g (12 oz) round grain pudding rice*
> *2 level teaspoons salt*
> *boiling water*
> *4 tablespoons olive oil*
> *175g (6 oz) onion chopped*
> *50g (2 oz) pine nuts*
> *25g (1 oz) currants*
> *125g (4 oz) skinned tomatoes, chopped*
> *2½cm (1 in) piece of cinnamon stick*
> *425ml (¾ pt) boiling water*
> *½ extra level teaspoon salt*

1. Place the rice in a bowl. Toss with salt. Cover with boiling water. Leave

the rice to stand until the water is completely cold. Drain the rice thoroughly. Leave on one side temporarily.

2. Meanwhile, heat the oil until sizzling in a large pan. Add the onions. Fry gently until pale gold. Stir in the nuts. Continue to fry for a few minutes until pale gold as well.

3. Replace the rice. Stir in all the remaining ingredients. Bring to the boil, stirring. Lower the heat. Cover. Simmer slowly for 45 minutes to 1 hour when the rice should be completely tender and have absorbed all the moisture. Serve with any cheese dish to taste or fried eggs. The Pilav also goes well with omelets.

Egg and Mushroom Layer Bake — serves 4 to 5

6 hard boiled eggs
½kg (1 lb) cold cooked potatoes
1 can condensed cream of mushroom soup
3 tablespoons milk
1 level tablespoon breadcrumbs
25g (1 oz) butter
paprika

1. Slice the eggs and potatoes. Heat the soup in a pan with the milk, whisking continuously, until completely smooth.

2. Fill a 1½l (2½ pt) well-buttered casserole dish with half the potatoes, all the eggs and half the soup.

3. Cover with the rest of the potatoes then coat with the remaining soup.

4. Sprinkle with breadcrumbs. Top with flakes of butter. Add a dusting of paprika.

5. Reheat and brown for 20 minutes in hot oven set to 220°C/425°F, Gas 7. Serve with coleslaw salad.

French Piperade — serves 4

350g (12 oz) onions, chopped
225g (8 oz) green peppers, de-seeded and chopped
75g (3 oz) butter
1 dessertspoon olive oil
½kg (1 lb) tomatoes, skinned and chopped
8 large eggs
5 tablespoons single cream
salt and freshly milled black pepper to taste

1. In a fairly large and sturdy frying pan, fry the onions and peppers in the butter and oil until golden. Keep the heat very low, the pan covered and allow about 15 to 20 minutes.

2. Add the tomatoes, mix in well and fry for a further 7 minutes.

3. Beat the eggs and cream together then season to taste with salt and freshly milled pepper.

4. Add to the vegetable mixture. Cook and stir over minimal heat until the eggs are lightly scrambled. Pile at once on to 4 warm plates and serve with crusty French bread and butter.

Sweet-Sour Beans with Egg Scramble — serves 4

½kg (1 lb) runner beans
275ml (½ pt) water
1 to 1½ level teaspoons salt
1 level tablespoon cornflour
1 tablespoon granulated sugar
2 tablespoons cider vinegar
1 garlic clove, crushed
6 large eggs
150ml (¼ pt) milk
large pinch nutmeg
salt and pepper to taste

1. Top and tail the beans. Remove side strings. Cut the beans into fairly thin diagonal slices.

2. Place in pan with 150ml (½ pt) water and the salt. Bring to the boil. Cover. Lower the heat and simmer until the beans are only *just* tender; they should not be allowed to overcook.

3. Mix the cornflour and sugar to a smooth cream with the vinegar. Add to the beans with the garlic. Cook, stirring all the time, until the mixture comes to the boil and thickens. Simmer for 2 minutes. Leave over minimal heat temporarily.

4. Beat the eggs with the rest of the ingredients and scramble lightly. Turn on to 4 plates and add a helping of sweet-sour beans to each.

Curried Lentils with Eggs — serves 4

1 tablespoon salad oil
125g (4 oz) onions, chopped
2 garlic cloves, finely chopped
1 rounded tablespoon curry powder (mild, medium or hot, according to taste)
225g (8 oz) lentils, washed
275ml (½ pt) water
1 tablespoon tubed or canned tomato concentrate
2 level teaspoons salt
4 hard boiled eggs

1.   Heat the oil in a heavy pan. Add the onions and garlic. Fry gently until pale gold.
2.   Stir in the curry powder, lentils, water, tomato concentrate and salt. Bring to the boil, stirring. Lower the heat. Cover.
3.   Cook gently for about 30 to 40 minutes or until the lentils are soft. Serve with hard boiled eggs. Accompany with roast potatoes and a salad of tomatoes with raw onions coated with French dressing and a sprinkling of cumin.

Cheesey Butter Bean and Cashew Casserole — serves 4 to 6

> *225g (8 oz) butter beans, soaked overnight*
> *cold water*
> *2 level teaspoons salt*
> *pinch soda bicarbonate*
> *225g (8 oz) onions, quartered*
> *25g (1 oz) butter*
> *25g (1 oz) flour*
> *425ml (¾ pt) milk*
> *175g (6 oz) mature Cheddar cheese*
> *75g (3 oz) toasted cashews*
> *salt and pepper to taste*

1.   Drain the beans. Put into a large pan with plenty of cold water. Add the salt and soda bicarbonate. Bring to the boil and cover. Lower the heat and cook gently for 1¼ hours.
2.   Add the onions and cook for a further 20 minutes. Drain. To make the sauce, melt the butter in a clean pan. Stir in the flour. Cook for 1 minute. Gradually blend in the milk.
3.   Cook, stirring, until the sauce comes to the boil and thickens. Add the butter beans, onions, two-thirds of the cheese and 50g (2 oz) cashews. Season to taste with salt and pepper.
4.   Transfer to a buttered heatproof dish. Sprinkle the rest of the cheese on top. Brown under a hot grill. Scatter the remaining cashews over the top. Serve with a crisp salad.

Three-Layer Country Pie — serves 4

> *½kg (1 lb) parsnips, washed and halved*
> *225g (8 oz) onions, washed and halved*
> *boiling salted water*
> *225g (8 oz) mature Cheddar cheese, grated*
> *salt and pepper*
> *275ml (½ pt) whipping cream*

1. Parboil the parsnips and onions in boiling salted water, allowing about 7 to 10 minutes. Drain. Leave the vegetables until lukewarm then cut into slices (not too thick).
2. Fill a 1½l (2½ pt) buttered heatproof dish with alternate layers of parsnips, onions and two-thirds of the cheese, sprinkling salt and pepper between the layers.
3. Pour the cream gently into the dish (down one side is the easiest). Sprinkle the rest of the cheese on top. Reheat and brown for 40 minutes in a moderately hot oven set to 200°C/400°F, Gas 6. Serve with a cooked green vegetable.

Ratatouille Rice — serves 6

> *4 tablespoons olive oil*
> *225g (8 oz) onions, thinly sliced*
> *2 garlic cloves, crushed*
> *½kg (1 lb) blanched tomatoes, skinned and chopped*
> *1 medium green pepper, de-seeded and chopped*
> *½kg (1 lb) topped and tailed courgettes, sliced*
> *1 large aubergine, topped and tailed*
> *1 to 1½ level teaspoons salt*
> *1 or 2 grindings freshly milled white pepper*
> *4 level tablespoons chopped parsley*
> *1 level teaspoon basil*

1. Heat the oil in a large and heavy-based pan. Add the onions and garlic. Fry slowly, with the lid on the pan, until soft and golden brown in colour.
2. Stir in the tomatoes, green pepper and courgettes.
3. *Do not peel* the aubergine but cut into slices and add to the pan with salt and the freshly milled pepper. Stir well. Cover.
4. Cook for about 1½ to 1¾ hours or until the vegetables are very soft, stirring occasionally.
5. Uncover, stir in the parsley and basil then simmer, with no lid, until the Ratatouille is fairly thick.
6. Spoon portions over the cooked rice (allowing about 50g (2 oz) per person) then sprinkle with grated Parmesan cheese.
Note
If preferred, the Ratatouille may be spooned over freshly-cooked pasta; I would recommend wholewheat spaghetti.

Baked Rainbow Eggs — serves 4

> *½kg (1 lb) topped and tailed courgettes*
> *½kg (1 lb) tomatoes, blanched and skinned*

salt and pepper
4 standard (grade 3) eggs
150ml (¼ pt) soured cream
2 tablespoons milk
125g (4 oz) Gruyère cheese, grated
1 rounded teaspoon poppy seeds

1.   Set the oven to moderately hot, 200°C/400°F, Gas 6. Well butter a shallow, oblong heatproof dish.
2.   Cut the courgettes into ⅝cm (¼ in) slices. Parboil in boiling, salted water for 5 minutes. Drain.
3.   Spread over the base of a buttered dish then top with the tomatoes, first thinly sliced.
4.   Season with salt and pepper to taste then break the eggs gently on top.
5.   Beat the soured cream and milk well together and spoon gently over the eggs.
6.   Sprinkle with grated cheese and poppy seeds then heat through and brown in the oven for about 20 minutes. Serve with freshly boiled rice forked with butter and a little dried tarragon.

Assorted Salads

Seashell Sparkle Salad — serves 4/5

> *225g (8 oz) shell-shaped pasta*
> *boiling salted water*
> *225g (8 oz) Edam cheese, cut into small dice*
> *125g (4 oz) raw mushrooms, trimmed and thinly sliced*
> *125g (4 oz) onions, very thinly sliced*
> *75g (3 oz) Brazil nuts, sliced*
> *6 level tablespoons cooked sweetcorn*
> *150ml (¼ pt) mayonnaise*

Garnish
cucumber and tomato slices

1. Cook the pasta as directed on the packet, allowing about 8 to 10 minutes. Drain. Rinse with cold water. Shake dry in a colander. Tip into a mixing bowl.
2. Add the diced cheese, the raw mushrooms, onion slices separated into rings, the nuts and sweetcorn. Toss thoroughly with mayonnaise.
3. Spoon neatly into a serving bowl and decorate with tomato and cucumber. Serve with split and freshly toasted bap rolls and butter.

Chestnut and Cranberry Salad — serves 4

75g (3 oz) fresh cranberries
3 level teaspoons caster sugar
1 can chestnuts in water (275g/10 oz drained weight)
½ level teaspoon salt
25g (1 oz) pecan nuts, coarsely chopped
1 dessert apple, diced
2 tablespoons lemon-flavoured mayonnaise
1 large orange, peeled and sliced

1. Place the cranberries on a board (take care as they roll easily) and cut each in half. Transfer to a mixing bowl. Add sugar.
2. Break up the drained chestnuts into fairly large pieces. Add to cranberries with all the remaining ingredients except the orange. Toss gently with a spoon until well mixed.
3. Garnish attractively with the orange slices, first cut in half. Serve with wedges of Port Salut cheese or, for a stronger flavour, French Roquefort. Accompany with small new potatoes tossed in butter.

Mexican Style Bean and Avocado Salad — serves 6

225g (8 oz) American long grain rice
575ml (1 pt) water
1 level teaspoon salt
1 can (about ½kg/1 lb) American red kidney beans, drained and rinsed
1 can (350g/12 oz) sweet corn kernels, drained
2 large avocados
1 small onion, grated
5 tablespoons French dressing
2 heaped tablespoons chopped parsley

1. Cook the rice in water and salt as directed on the packet. It should take about 12 to 15 minutes and the pan should be kept covered. Leave until cold.
2. Tip the rice into a large mixing bowl. Add the beans and sweet corn. Peel the avocados as you would peel a pear, starting from the pointed end. Cut into dice. Add to the bowl with the onion and French dressing. Toss thoroughly.
3. Spoon the salad neatly into a bowl and sprinkle with the parsley. Serve with omelets.

Aubergine Rice Salad — serves 4

1kg (2 lb) aubergines
4 tablespoons lemon juice

1 small onion, grated
125g (4 oz) American long grain rice, cooked and left to cool
2 tablespoons olive oil
1 to 1½ level teaspoons salt

Garnish
wedges of tomato

1.   Grill the aubergines under a very high heat for about 20 minutes or until the skin is charred and the flesh feels tender when gently squeezed. Turn frequently for even cooking.
2.   Rinse the aubergines under cold, running water, removing the skins at the same time. Put the aubergines into a colander. Squeeze hard against the sides to remove as much surplus moisture as possible.
3.   Transfer to a chopping board. Sprinkle with half the lemon juice. Chop fairly finely. Transfer to a mixing bowl. Stir in all the remaining ingredients.
4.   Arrange neatly in a serving dish and garnish with tomatoes. Accompany with a mild cheese such as Caerphilly.
Note
Instead of grilling, aubergines may be baked in a moderately hot oven (220°C/400°F, Gas 6) for 20 minutes.

Peridot Salad — serves 4

225g (8 oz) bean sprouts, washed and drained thoroughly
3 medium celery stalks
1 large avocado
4 tablespoons salad oil
1 level teaspoon French mustard
1 small onion, grated
shake or two of Tabasco
2 rounded teaspoons canned green peppers (from Madagascar; used for pepper steaks)
½ level teaspoon salt
2 tablespoons wine vinegar

1.   Place the bean sprouts in a large mixing bowl. Slice the well-washed celery fairly thinly. Peel the avocado as you would peel a pear, starting from the pointed end. Cut the flesh into dice. Add the celery and avocado dice to the bean sprouts in the bowl.
2.   Beat the oil with the next 3 ingredients. Stir in the peppers and salt. Whisk in the vinegar. Add to the vegetables. Toss well. Transfer to a serving bowl. Serve with hot pasta stirred round with plenty of butter and sprinkled with grated Parmesan cheese.

Tomatoes with Creamed Chive Dressing — serves 4

½kg (1 lb) tomatoes, sliced
1 packet (75g/3 oz) Philadelphia cream cheese with chopped chives
3 tablespoons single cream
½ level teaspoon salt
½ large green pepper, washed and finely chopped

1.   Arrange the tomatoes over the base of a dinner plate. Beat the cheese with the cream and salt.
2.   When smooth and thin enough for coating (you might have to add an extra tablespoon of cream or milk), spoon over the tomatoes.
3.   Garnish by sprinkling with the green pepper. Serve with a savoury soufflé and sauté potatoes.

Thousand Island Salad — serves 4

½ small lettuce, leaves washed and patted dry with paper towels
1 small cucumber, thinly sliced (do not peel)
1 medium onion (Spanish for mildness), thinly sliced
3 rounded tablespoons cooked peas
½ large green pepper, cut into strips
3 level tablespoons Thousand Island dressing

1.   Arrange the lettuce over the base of a serving bowl that is not too deep.
2.   Put the cucumber into a mixing bowl. Add the onion slices, first separated into rings, together with the peas, green pepper and dressing.
3.   Toss well to mix and pile on to the lettuce. Serve with an assorted cheese board. Also biscuits and butter.

Paradise Salad — serves 4

6 large red peppers
boiling water

6 large hard boiled eggs, shelled when cold
175g (6 oz) onions
2 heaped tablespoons chopped parsley

Dressing
4 tablespoons salad oil
1 level teaspoon German mustard
1 level teaspoon celery salt
1 level teaspoon salt
shake of white pepper
2 level tablespoons lemon juice

1.   Wash the peppers. Cut off the tops and remove the inside fibres and seeds. Discard. Put the peppers into a large saucepan. Cover with boiling water. Cover. Boil gently for 10 minutes. Drain thoroughly. Leave until cold.
2.   Cut the peppers into thin strips and put into a mixing bowl. Coarsely grate the eggs directly over the peppers. Peel the onions and slice. Separate the slices into rings. Add to the bowl with the parsley.
3.   For the dressing, beat the oil with the mustard, both salts and pepper. Add the lemon juice. Whisk until the dressing thickens.
4.   Pour into the bowl over the pepper mixture. Toss with 2 spoons. Transfer to a salad bowl. Accompany with brown bread and butter.

Sunshine Salad — serves 6

½kg (1 lb) white cabbage
6 medium celery stalks
1 medium trimmed leek, slit and well washed
225g (8 oz) red Cheshire cheese
125g (4 oz) finely chopped dates
2 large grapefruit
about 5 tablespoons mayonnaise

Garnish
2 medium carrots, very finely grated
4 hard boiled eggs, cut into wedges

1.   Shred the cabbage finely. Thinly slice the celery and leek. Cut the Cheshire cheese into dice.
2.   Place the prepared vegetables into a mixing bowl then add the cheese and dates.
3.   Peel the grapefruit, removing all traces of white pith. Cut the flesh into dice. Add to the salad bowl. Toss with mayonnaise.
4.   Transfer the salad to a serving bowl then top with mounds of grated carrot. Arrange the eggs attractively on top. Serve with hot buttered toast.

Winter Opal Salad — serves 5 to 6

1 medium head celery
1kg (2 lb) Chinese leaves
2 heads Belgian chicory, washed
1 bag (about 150g/5 oz) radishes, washed

Dressing
4 tablespoons salad oil
2 large garlic cloves, crushed
½ level teaspoon dry mustard
1 teaspoon Worcester sauce
1 or 2 shakes Tabasco
1 level teaspoon salt
1 level teaspoon caster sugar
2 tablespoons vinegar

1. Wash and scrub the celery stalks and remove any coarse strings. Cut into thin, diagonal strips. Put into a bowl.
2. Wash and dry the Chinese leaves and shred. Remove the 'cores' from the base of each chicory head (this part is very bitter and best discarded). Thinly slice the heads with a stainless knife. Slice the radishes. Add all three vegetables to the celery.
3. To make the dressing, beat the oil with the next 6 ingredients. Gradually whisk in the vinegar. When the dressing thickens, pour over the salad and toss well with 2 spoons.
Note
If covered with cling film or foil and refrigerated, the salad stays crisp for about 24 hours.

Lemony Carrot Salad — Serves 4-6

½kg (1 lb) raw carrots, finely shredded
4 rounded tablespoons seedless raisins
lemon juice to taste
salt and pepper to taste

Garnish
chopped walnuts

1. Toss carrots with raisins, add lemon juice to taste.
2. Season to taste with salt and pepper.
3. Pile in to a serving bowl and sprinkle top lightly with walnuts.
4. Cover and chill for about 30 minutes before serving.

Winter Iceberg Salad — serves 4

1 winter iceberg lettuce (from Israel), washed and shaken dry
1 packet (150g/5 oz) radishes, trimmed and sliced
1 large red pepper, halved and de-seeded
4 large celery stalks, washed and thinly sliced
2 large oranges
4 tablespoons salad oil
1 level tablespoon clear honey
1 level teaspoon prepared mild mustard
1 teaspoon Worcester sauce
1 level teaspoon onion salt
2 tablespoons lemon juice

Garnish
a few celery leaves

1.   Shred the lettuce and put into a large mixing bowl. Add the radishes. Cut the pepper into thin strips. Add to the bowl with the celery.
2.   Peel the oranges, removing all traces of pith. Cut into small dice. Stir into the salad vegetables.
3.   To make the dressing, beat the oil with all the remaining ingredients except lemon juice. When thoroughly blended, whisk in lemon juice and continue whisking until the dressing thickens.
4.   Add to the salad and toss thoroughly with 2 spoons. Transfer to a salad bowl and garnish with celery leaves. Serve with Greek style Feta cheese or ripe Camembert. Brown rolls and butter makes an acceptable accompaniment.

Greek Feta Cheese and Olive Salad — serves 4 to 6

> *1 large garlic clove, halved*
> *1 round lettuce*
> *1 medium peeled cucumber*
> *2 medium onions, peeled*
> *1 medium green pepper, halved and de-seeded*
> *225g (8 oz) blanched tomatoes, skinned*
> *3 tablespoons French dressing*
> *75g (3 oz) Greek black olives*
> *175g (6 oz) Feta cheese*
> *olive oil*

1.   Crush the garlic clove against the sides of a salad bowl in order to extract the flavour without necessarily incorporating pieces of garlic in the salad. Discard bits.
2.   Wash the lettuce thoroughly. Drain well. Wipe the leaves dry on paper towels, taking care not to bruise them.
3.   Shred the lettuce with a stainless knife and add to the bowl. Thinly slice the cucumber. Repeat with the onion then separate each slice into rings. Cut the pepper into strips. Cut the tomatoes into wedges. Add all the prepared vegetables to the bowl.
4.   Add the dressing and toss. Sprinkle with olives then top with Feta cheese, cut into thinnish pieces. Trickle with olive oil. Serve with Pita bread.

Curried Rice Salad — serves 4

> *225g (8 oz) Basmati rice*
> *575ml (1 pt) boiling water*
> *1 level teaspoon salt*
> *3 to 4 level teaspoons mild or hot curry powder, depending on taste*
> *2 level teaspoons garam masala*
> *3 cardamon seeds*
> *1 bay leaf*
> *½ cinnamon stick*
> *1 garlic clove, crushed*
> *3 level tablespoons mango chutney*

> **Topping**
> *1 large onion, sliced*
> *3 hardboiled eggs, cut into wedges*
> *4 large tomatoes, cut into thin wedges*

1.   Place the rice into a heavy-based saucepan. Add all the remaining

ingredients. Stir well to mix. Bring to the boil. Stir round again. Lower heat and cover.

2.   Cook for about 20 minutes or until the rice grains are separate and have absorbed all the moisture. Fork-stir round again, tip into a bowl and leave until completely cold. Remove the bay leaf and cinnamon stick.

3.   Arrange the rice over a serving dish. Decorate with sliced onion (first separated into rings), lines of egg wedges and the tomatoes.

Hot Spice Rice — serves 4

Make exactly as above but transfer freshly cooked rice to 4 warm plates. Top with freshly fried eggs and serve with side dishes of chopped onions, chopped tomatoes and extra chutney.

Jewel Salad — serves 4

175g (6 oz) red cabbage, very finely shredded
125g (4 oz) carrot, grated
1 medium cucumber, unpeeled and diced
½ medium red pepper, de-seeded and shredded
½ medium green pepper, de-seeded and shredded
75g (3 oz) small black olives
6 to 8 tablespoons French dressing
4 heaped tablespoons Polish style gherkins, grated

1.   Combine all the ingredients, except the gherkins, well together. Toss thoroughly.

2.   Spoon neatly into a salad bowl and decorate with mounds of grated gherkin.

Cauliflower and Green Pepper Salad — serves 4

1 round lettuce
½ large or 1 medium cauliflower, trimmed of greenery
1 large green pepper, halved and de-seeded
25g (1 oz) chopped dates
5 tablespoons French dressing
2 heaped tablespoons chopped parsley

1.   Wash the lettuce and shake the leaves dry. Use the outer ones to line a salad bowl.

2.   Shred the lettuce heart with a stainless knife. Break the cauliflower into small florets. Chop the green pepper fairly finely. Place the prepared vegetables in a mixing bowl.

3.   Add the dates and dressing. Toss thoroughly. Spoon into the lettuce-lined bowl. Sprinkle with chopped parsley.

Middle European Sauerkraut Salad — serves 4

225g (8 oz) well-drained canned or bottled sauerkraut
175g (6 oz) carrots, finely grated
1 medium red pepper, de-seeded and cut into fine strips
1 small onion, grated
2 tablespoons lemon juice
3 tablespoons salad oil
salt and pepper to taste

1. Place the first 4 ingredients into a mixing bowl. Toss with the lemon juice and oil.
2. Season to taste with salt and pepper and transfer to a salad bowl. Serve with eggs or cheese.

Finnish Pineapple Salad — serves 8

1 medium pineapple
1kg (2 lb) cold, cooked potatoes, diced
225g (8 oz) carrots, grated
2 tablespoons lemon juice
275ml (½ pt) double cream
1 tablespoon milk
salt and pepper to taste

1. Peel the pineapple, removing the eyes with an apple peeler. Cut the fruit into slices. Remove the hard cores from the centres of the slices then cut the flesh into small pieces.
2. Put into a mixing bowl with the potatoes, two-thirds of the carrots and the lemon juice. Mix well.
3. Beat the cream and milk together until thick. Season to taste with salt and pepper. Fold into the salad ingredients, tossing over and over.
4. Transfer to a salad bowl and garnish with the remaining carrot. Serve with omelets and scrambled eggs.

Hot Celeriac 'Salad' — serves 4 to 6

¾kg (1½ lb) celeriac
cold water
1 to 1½ level teaspoons salt
1 tablespoon lemon juice
5 tablespoons French dressing
1 dessertspoon drained capers, finely chopped
2 heaped tablespoons chopped parsley
1 level teaspoon mixed herbs
1 small onion, grated

1.   Peel the celeriac and slice. Place in a pan. Cover with cold water. Add salt and lemon juice. Cook, covered, until tender but not over soft and check after ¼ hour.
2.   Drain thoroughly. Place in a mixing bowl and add all the remaining ingredients. Toss with 2 spoons. Transfer to a warm dish. Serve with nut burgers or omelets.

Broad Bean Salad — serves 4 to 5

> *½kg (1 lb) broad beans (shelled weight)*
> *boiling salted water*
> *1 small onion, grated*
> *4 heaped tablespoons chopped parsley*
> *2 level teaspoons chopped mint*
> *3 tablespoons olive oil*
> *1 level teaspoon prepared French mustard*
> *1 or 2 shakes Tabasco*
> *¼ level teaspoon salt*
> *pinch of caster sugar*
> *1½ tablespoons lemon juice*
> *1 hard boiled egg, chopped*
> *25g (1 oz) almond nibs, lightly fried in butter*

1.   Cook the beans in boiling salted water for between 15 and 20 minutes or until tender. Drain thoroughly. Leave until completely cold.
2.   Put into a bowl, add the next 3 ingredients and mix well. To make the dressing, beat the oil with the mustard, Tabasco, salt and sugar. Whisk in the lemon juice.
3.   Add the dressing to the beans and toss well with 2 spoons. Cover and refrigerate for about 2 hours before serving. Transfer to a dish and sprinkle with chopped egg and almonds.

Tunisian Mechouia (Mixed Salad) — serves 4

> *1 medium red pepper*
> *1 medium green pepper*
> *salted water*
> *350g (12 oz) blanched tomatoes, skinned*
> *125g (4 oz) onion, finely grated*
> *1 small garlic clove, chopped*
> *2 rounded teaspoons drained capers, finely chopped*
> *4 tablespoons olive oil*
> *1 level teaspoon salt*
> *shake of white pepper*
> *2 tablespoons lemon juice*

1. De-seed the peppers and cut the flesh into strips. Boil for 5 minutes in salted water. Drain *thoroughly*. Chop finely. Leave until completely cold. Put into a mixing bowl.
2. Chop the tomatoes finely, discarding seeds. Add to the bowl with the onion, garlic and capers.
3. Beat the oil with the salt and pepper. Gradually beat in the lemon juice. Pour over the salad. Toss well to mix. Pile onto individual plates.

Macaroni Hazelnut Salad — serves 4 to 6

> *175g (6 oz) elbow macaroni*
> *3 tablespoons salad oil*
> *1 tablespoon lemon juice*
> *1 level teaspoon paprika*
> *½ large unpeeled cucumber, diced*
> *75g (3 oz) Caerphilly cheese, diced*
> *50g (2 oz) hazelnuts*
> *½ level teaspoon onion salt*
> *1 level tablespoon finely chopped parsley*
> *1 large carrot, grated*
> *salt and pepper to taste*

1. Cook the macaroni in boiling salted water as directed on the packet. Allow about 8 to 10 minutes. *Do not* overcook or the macaroni will become soggy and bloated.
2. Tip into a colander and rinse under cold water. Leave to drain thoroughly.
3. Tip into a mixing bowl. Add all the remaining ingredients and toss well with two spoons. Arrange in a lettuce-lined serving bowl.

Rosyglow Salad — serves 6

> *225g (8 oz) red cabbage*
> *½kg (1 lb) green cabbage*
> *50g (2 oz) sultanas*
> *125g (4 oz) slightly under-ripe Brie cheese, cubed*
> *2 large bananas*
> *2 medium dessert apples*
> *1 medium dessert pear*
> *6 tablespoons French dressing*

1. Wash the cabbage thoroughly and drain. Finely shred both varieties and put into a large mixing bowl.
2. Add the sultanas, Brie cheese and sliced bananas.

3.   Wash and dry the apples and pear. Do not peel but remove the cores. Dice the flesh.
4.   Add to the bowl of cabbage etc and toss with the dressing.
5.   Serve with wholemeal bread and butter and extra portions of Brie cheese.

Yugoslavian Tomato and Green Pepper Salad — serves 6

> ½kg (1 lb) tomatoes, blanched and skinned
> 2 medium green peppers
> 125g (4 oz) onions
> 3 level tablespoons chopped parsley
> 1 level teaspoon caster sugar
> 1 level teaspoon salt
> 4 tablespoons French dressing

1.   Thinly slice the tomatoes. Halve the green peppers and remove the inside fibres and seeds. Cut the flesh into thin strips. Cut the onions into wafer thin slices then separate the slices into rings.
2.   Put all the prepared vegetables into a bowl. Add parsley, sugar and salt to taste. Add French dressing.
3.   Toss gently. Cover. Refrigerate for about 30 minutes. Serve with omelets or scrambled egg.
Note
This salad is equally good with Greek Feta cheese or large wedges of slightly under-ripe Brie or Camembert.

Hot and Cold Desserts

Old Fashioned Syrup Tart — serves 6

shortcrust pastry made with 225g (8 oz) plain flour

Filling
350g (12 oz) golden syrup
25g (1 oz) butter
50g (2 oz) fresh white breadcrumbs
finely grated peel and juice of 1 small lemon

1.   Set the oven to moderately hot, 200°C/400°F, Gas 6. Well butter a fairly shallow metal tart plate with a rim measuring 20cm (8 in) in diameter.
2.   Roll out two-thirds of the pastry fairly thinly on a floured surface. Use to line the tart plate, making sure the pastry covers the rim of the plate. Do not stretch the pastry as it will shrink back as it bakes.
3.   Pour the syrup into a pan. Add the butter and stir over a low heat until melted. Stir in all the remaining ingredients and mix well.
4.   Cool slightly. Spread over the pastry base but do not cover the rim. Moisten the rim with a brush dipped in cold water. Roll out the rest of the pastry. Cut into strips.
5.   Criss-cross the strips over the tart, twisting each as you do so. Press the ends into the pastry rim so that they form a seal and stay in place.

6. Bake for 25 to 35 minutes when the tart should be golden brown. Cut into wedges and serve in traditional fashion with single cream or custard.
Note
For a spicy tart, add ½ to 1 level teaspoon cinnamon with crumbs.

Chocolate Fingers with Creme de Menthe Cream — serves 6

200g (7 oz) self raising flour
25g (1 oz) cocoa powder
125g (4 oz) butter
75g (3 oz) soft brown sugar
2 level tablespoons black treacle
1 large egg, beaten
1 teaspoon vanilla essence
about 4 tablespoons cold milk to mix

Creme de Menthe Cream
150ml (¼ pt) double cream
1 tablespoon milk
2 tablespoons green Creme de Menthe

1. Grease and line with greaseproof paper a Swiss roll tin measuring 17½cm x 27½cm x 2½cm (7 x 11 x 1 in). Brush the paper with melted butter. Set the oven to moderately hot, 190°C/375°F, Gas 5.
2. Sift the flour and cocoa powder into a bowl. Rub in the butter finely. Toss in sugar.
3. Using a fork, mix to a softish batter with the rest of the ingredients.
4. When smooth and evenly combined, spread into prepared tin. Bake for about 30 to 40 minutes or until well-risen and firm. Remove from the oven. Cut into 12 fingers.
5. Place 2 fingers on each of 6 plates then pass the Creme de Menthe Cream separately. To make, beat the cream with the milk and Creme de Menthe until softly stiff. Swirl into a dish and add a serving spoon.

Honey and Banana Pudding with Rum Cream — serves 4

50g (2 oz) clear honey
1 large banana
125g (4 oz) self raising flour
50g (2 oz) butter, softened
50g (2 oz) caster sugar
1 standard egg
2 tablespoons milk

Rum Cream
150ml (¼ pt) double cream

1 level tablespoon caster sugar
1 tablespoon dark rum

1.   Well butter a 1¼l (2 pt) pie dish. Cover the base with honey and sliced banana.
2.   Sift the flour into a bowl. Rub in the butter finely. Toss in sugar. Using a fork, mix to a semi-stiff batter with the unbeaten egg and milk.
3.   Spread smoothly into the dish over the honey and banana. Bake for about 30 to 40 minutes in a moderate oven set to 180°C/350°F, Gas 4. After this time, the pudding should be well risen and golden.
4.   Carefully invert on to a warm dish and accompany with the rum cream, made by beating the cream until softly stiff with the sugar and rum.

Zabaglione with Brandied Peaches — serves 6

3 medium peaches, blanched and skinned
3 tablespoons brandy
3 standard (grade 3) eggs
3 egg yolks
125g (4 oz) caster sugar
4 tablespoons Marsala

1.   Halve the peaches, remove stones, and place in 6 glass bowls or dishes. Sprinkle with brandy. Leave on one side temporarily.
2.   To make the Zabaglione, place all the ingredients into large basin standing over pan of gently simmering water.
3.   Whisk continuously until the mixture becomes light and airy and takes on the appearance of softly whipped cream. This could take anything from 7 to 12 minutes.
4.   Spoon into the dishes over the brandied peaches and serve straight away with crisp, sweet biscuits.

Gingerbread Squares with Apple and Raisin Sauce — serves 6

175g (6 oz) plain flour
2 level teaspoons ground ginger
1 level teaspoon mixed spice
½ level teaspoon soda bicarbonate
75g (3 oz) golden syrup
1 slightly rounded tablespoon orange marmalade
1 level tablespoon black treacle
25g (1 oz) butter
25g (1 oz) caster sugar
1 standard egg
2 tablespoons milk

Apple and Raisin Sauce

> ½kg (1 lb) apples (juicy cookers)
> 3 tablespoons water
> 3 to 4 tablespoons clear honey
> 50g (2 oz) seedless raisins

1.   Set the oven to moderate, 180°C/350°F, Gas 4. Butter and paper-line a tin measuring 15cm (6 in) square.
2.   Sift the dry ingredients into a bowl. Put the syrup, marmalade, treacle, butter and sugar into saucepan. Stand over a low heat and leave until the butter melts.
3.   Make a well in the centre of the dry ingredients. Pour in the syrup mixture then add the egg, beaten well with the milk.
4.   Using a fork, stir briskly without beating. When smooth and evenly combined, pour into the tin and spread the top evenly with a knife.
5.   Bake in the centre of the oven for 45 minutes until firm and golden or until a skewer, pushed gently into the centre, comes out clean with no uncooked pieces of mixture clinging to it.
6.   Leave in the tin for 10 minutes then turn out on to a dish. Peel away the paper, cut into 6 portions and top each with hot apple and raisin sauce.
7.   To make the sauce, peel and core the apples. Slice thinly. Put into a saucepan with water.
8.   Cook, over a low heat, until soft and pulpy. Keep the pan covered throughout. Stir occasionally. Finally, stir in the honey and raisins.

American Pumpkin Pie — serves 8

> about 1¾kg (3½ lb) pumpkin (½ medium)
> 1 level tablespoon black treacle
> 175g (6 oz) soft brown sugar (light variety)
> 15g (½ oz) cornflour
> 3 level teaspoons mixed spice
> 150ml (¼ pt) canned evaporated milk (unsweetened)
> 3 standard (grade 3) eggs
> 225g (8 oz) shortcrust pastry, made with 225g (8 oz) plain flour

1.   Set the oven to moderate, 180°C/400°F, Gas 4. Well-butter a baking tray. Remove the seeds and strings from the centre of the pumpkin. Stand on the baking tray, skin side uppermost.
2.   Bake for 1½ hours or until the flesh is *very* soft. Remove from the oven and scoop the flesh into a bowl. Mash finely. Tie in a clean teatowel, twist the ends and squeeze hard to remove as much moisture as possible; you should be left with about ½kg (1 lb) dry pumpkin pulp.
3.   Transfer the pumpkin to a bowl and beat in the treacle, sugar, cornflour, mixed spice, evaporated milk and the eggs.

4.   Roll out the pastry fairly thinly and use to line a 25cm (10 in) flan ring standing on a buttered baking tray. Fill with the pumpin mixture.

5.   Bake for about 45 to 55 minutes in moderately hot oven set to 200°C/400°F, Gas 6. At this stage the filling should be set (like a custard mixture), and the pastry pale golden-brown.

6.   Remove from the oven. Cool to lukewarm. Lift off the flan ring. Transfer the pie to a large serving platter. Cut into large wedges and serve while still warm with softly whipped cream.

American Style Strawberry 'Shortcakes' — serves 4

225g (8 oz) self raising flour
pinch salt
50g (2 oz) butter
25g (1 oz) caster sugar
8 tablespoons single cream

Filling
225g (8 oz) fresh strawberries, sliced
2 level tablespoons caster sugar
50g (2 oz) butter

Topping
150ml (¼ pt) double cream
1 tablespoon milk
1 tablespoon apricot brandy

1.   Set the oven to moderately hot, 200°C/400°F, Gas 6. Well butter a baking tray.

2.   Sift the flour and salt into a bowl. Rub in the butter finely. Toss in sugar. Mix to a soft dough with the cream.

3.   Turn out on to a floured surface and knead lightly until smooth. Roll out to 2½cm (1 in) in thickness. Cut into 4 rounds with a 7½cm (3 in) fluted biscuit cutter. Bake until well-risen and golden — about 15 to 20 minutes.

4.   Meanwhile, toss the strawberries and sugar well together. Cool the Shortcakes to lukewarm then split by pulling gently apart with the fingers. Butter fairly thickly.
5.   Sandwich together with the strawberries. Beat the cream and milk well together. Stir in the apricot brandy. Pile equal amounts onto each Shortcake. Serve while still just warm.

Fruit and Nut Orange Pudding — serves 8

350g (12 oz) self raising flour
1 level teaspoon salt
1 level teaspoon cinnamon
½ level teaspoon ginger
½ level teaspoon allspice
50g (2 oz) cooking dates, finely chopped
75g (3 oz) walnuts, finely chopped
75g (3 oz) soft brown sugar (light variety)
2 level teaspoons finely grated orange peel
2 standard eggs, beaten
275ml (½ pt) less 1 tablespoon cold tea, strained
50g (2 oz) butter, melted

1.   Set the oven to moderate, 180°C/350°F, Gas 4. Brush a 1kg (2 lb) loaf tin with melted butter. Line the base and sides with greaseproof paper. Brush the paper with more melted butter.
2.   Sift the flour, salt and spices into a bowl. Toss in the dates, walnuts, sugar and orange peel.
3.   Using a fork, blend in the eggs and tea, stirring briskly without beating. Gently fold in the butter.
4.   Transfer the mixture to the prepared tin and bake for about 1 hour or until well-risen and golden brown.
5.   Leave in the tin for about 5 minutes. Turn out and cool on a wire rack. Remove the paper and cut the pudding into 8 portions. Serve with vanilla ice cream.

Brandied Mincemeat Pudding — serves 4 to 5

225g (8 oz) mincemeat
2 tablespoons brandy
175g (6 oz) self raising flour
1 level teaspoon mixed spice
75g (3 oz) butter
75g (3 oz) soft brown sugar (light variety)
1 standard egg, beaten

½ level teaspoon almond essence
5 tablespoons milk

1.   Set the oven to moderately hot, 190°C/375°F, Gas 5. Well butter a 1¼l (2 pt) oval pie dish.
2.   Cover the base with mincemeat combined with the brandy.
3.   Sift the flour and spice into a bowl. Rub in the butter finely. Toss in sugar.
4.   Using a fork, mix to a softish batter with the egg, almond essence and milk.
5.   Spread smoothly over the mincemeat then bake the pudding until well-risen and golden allowing about ¾ hour. Invert on to a plate, cut into portions and serve hot with whipped cream.

Crunchy Topped Rhubarb and Lemon Pie — serves 4

½kg (1 lb) trimmed rhubarb, cut into 1¼cm (½ in) pieces
2 slightly rounded tablespoons golden syrup
3 tablespoons hot water

Topping
125g (4 oz) plain flour
25g (1 oz) porridge oats
65g (2½ oz) butter
50g (2 oz) soft brown sugar
finely grated peel of 1 small lemon

1.   Pre-heat the oven to moderate, 180°C/350°F, Gas 4. Well butter a 1¼l (2 pt) pie dish.
2.   Put the rhubarb into a dish then add the golden syrup mixed with the water. Stir thoroughly.
3.   Sift the flour into a bowl. Add the oats. Rub in the butter finely then toss in the brown sugar and lemon peel. Spread thickly over the rhubarb mixture. Bake for about 35 to 40 minutes when the topping should be golden brown and the rhubarb cooked. Serve hot with custard sauce or single cream.
Note
As the liquid is liable to leak out of the pie, I suggest you stand the dish on a baking tray to catch the drips.

Spanish Torrijas — serves 4

6 large slices white bread, with crusts removed
6 tablespoons milk
2 standard eggs, beaten
6 tablespoons olive oil for frying

For sprinkling
   2 level tablespoons caster sugar
   1 level teaspoon cinnamon

1.   Cut each slice of bread into 3 fingers. Dip first in milk and then in egg.
2.   Fry a few at a time in the hot olive oil until golden, turning once. Drain thoroughly on paper towels. Sprinkle well with the sugar first mixed with cinnamon. Serve while still hot.

Austrian Poppy Seed Cake — serves about 16

This is such an extraordinary cake, that I think it merits a word or two of explanation. It is charcoal grey in colour with a somewhat gritty texture. It sinks on cooling — but it's meant to. It is a treasured speciality from the Mozart city of Salzburg and I was only able to get the recipe because I knew somebody who knew somebody who knew somebody — the usual story. It makes a fascinating dessert and a good talking point, hence its inclusion. The ingredients are expensive so please don't be tempted to make the cake unless you are sure that those around you appreciate a touch of novelty.

   225g (8 oz) unsalted butter, (kitchen temperature and on the soft side)
   400g (14 oz) caster sugar
   finely grated peel of 2 small lemons
   1½ teaspoons vanilla essence
   7 standard (grade 3) eggs, separated
   400g (14 oz) dark grey poppy seeds (try delicatessens and/or health food shops)
   200g (7 oz) hazelnuts or walnuts, very finely ground
   125g (4 oz) chopped mixed peel
   50g (2 oz) seedless raisins
   50g (2 oz) sultanas

1.   Butter a 20cm (8 in) spring pan form (with clip-on sides). Line the base and sides with greaseproof paper. Brush the paper with melted butter.
2.   Set the oven to moderate, 180°C/350°F, Gas 4. Cream the butter with half the sugar, lemon peel and vanilla until very light and creamy and the consistency of softly whipped cream.
3.   Beat in the egg yolks and then stir in the poppy seeds, nuts, peel, raisins and sultanas. Beat the egg whites to a stiff snow. Gradually add half the remaining sugar and continue beating until the meringue is even stiffer than before and stands in high peaks when the beaters are lifted out of the bowl. Stir in the remaining sugar.
4.   Fold the meringue into the poppy seed mixture with a large metal spoon. Spread evenly into the prepared tin. Bake for 1 hour. Remove from the oven and cool completely in the tin. Unclip the sides and peel away the

lining paper with great care. Leave the cake on its metal base as it will break if you try to shift it.

5. Cut into wedges and serve just as it is — it is fairly rich and requires no embellishments.

Austrian Poppy Seed Cake with Rum — serves about 16

As soon as cake has been removed from the oven and is still hot, pour over 2 to 3 tablespoons dark rum.

Plum Compôte with Cointreau — serves 4

> *½kg (1 lb) well-washed cooking plums, halved and stoned*
> *4 tablespoons water*
> *finely grated peel and juice of 1 large orange*
> *3 level tablespoons granulated sugar*
> *2 tablespoons Cointreau*

1. Put the plums into a pan. Add water together with the grated orange peel and orange juice. Slowly bring to the boil, stirring.
2. Lower the heat. Cover. Cook very gently for about 10 minutes or until the plums are soft. Add the sugar. Stir over a low heat until dissolved. Cool completely.
3. Cover. Chill thoroughly by leaving in the refrigerator for about 2 to 3 hours. Just before serving, add the Cointreau. If liked, accompany with a jug of single cream.

Apricot Yogurt Amaretto — serves 4 to 6

> *575g (1¼ lb) plain yogurt*
> *225g (8 oz) fresh and ripe apricots, halved and stoned*
> *2 level tablespoons clear honey*
> *2 tablespoons Amaretto di Saronno*

> **Decoration**
> *50g (2 oz) blanched and toasted almonds, cut into slivers*

1. Pour the yogurt into a bowl. Chop the apricots into fairly small pieces. Add to the yogurt with the honey and Amaretto di Saronno.
2. Stir well and cover. Refrigerate for about 2 hours.
3. Before serving, stir round and spoon into individual dishes. Sprinkle each with almonds.

Lemon Rice Cream — serves 4

> *575ml (1 pt) milk*
> *2 level tablespoons caster sugar*

50g (2 oz) round grain pudding rice
the peel of ½ medium lemon
1 egg yolk
150ml (¼ pt) double cream
cinnamon

1. Pour the milk into a heavy-based saucepan and heat to lukewarm. Add the sugar and stir over a low heat until melted. Add the rice and lemon peel. Cover.
2. Cook *very gently* until the rice is soft and has absorbed most of the liquid. It should not, however, be completely dry and stirring occasionally is advisable to prevent burning.
3. Cool the mixture for about 10 minutes then remove and discard the lemon peel. Beat the egg yolk with 2 tablespoons of cream.
4. Stir into the rice mixture.
5. Divide between 4 dishes and, when completely cold, chill in the refrigerator for a minimum of 2 hours.
6. Whip the rest of the cream until softly stiff (if liked, sweeten by adding 1 level tablespoon caster sugar) and pile equal amounts on top of the cold rice pudding. Sprinkle with cinnamon. Serve with stewed fruit.

Autumn Fruit Salad with Mead — serves 6

225g (8 oz) each black and green grapes
4 tablespoons mead
2 tablespoons lemon juice
3 large bananas
25g (1 oz) blanched and split almonds, toasted

1. Halve the grapes and remove the pips. Place in a glass serving bowl. Toss with the mead and lemon juice.
2. Cover. Chill in the refrigerator for about 4 hours. Just before serving, slice in the bananas. Toss gently to mix. Sprinkle almonds over the top.

West Country Summer Junket — serves 4

575ml (1 pt) pasteurized milk
1 level tablespoon caster sugar
1 teaspoon vanilla essence
1 teaspoon essence of rennet
225g (8 oz) fresh strawberries
icing sugar to taste
2 tablespoons port

To serve
clotted or whipped cream

1.   Pour the milk into a saucepan. Add the sugar. Stir over a low heat until the sugar dissolves and the milk is lukewarm (blood heat). To test, dip in your small finger. If the milk is the correct temperature, it should strike you as neither hot nor cold.
2.   Remove from the heat. Stir in the vanilla essence and rennet. Stir round to mix well. Pour into 4 individual dishes, leaving a 2½cm (1 in) gap at top of each. Leave in the warm to set, then cover and refrigerate for 2 to 3 hours.
3.   Crush the strawberries with a fork. Sweeten to taste with icing sugar then stir in the port. Spoon gently over the junket in the dishes. Pass a bowl, or jug of cream separately.

Italian Oranges — serves 8

> *8 large oranges*
> *225g (8 oz) caster sugar*
> *275ml (½ pt) water*
> *2 tablespoons orange flavoured liqueur*

1.   Peel the oranges. Reserve the peel from three. Cut away the white pith from the peeled oranges and reserved peel.
2.   Cut the peel into very fine strips. Transfer to a saucepan and cover with water. Bring to the boil and cover. Simmer gently for ¼ hour. Drain and leave on one side temporarily.
3.   Put the sugar and water into a clean pan. Cook and stir over a gentle heat until the sugar dissolves. Bring to the boil. Making sure the syrup does not rise up in the pan and flow over the sides, continue to boil steadily until it starts to thicken. Do not stir and make sure the syrup does not start to change colour and turn pale gold. Cool to lukewarm. Add the liqueur.
4.   Add the oranges and toss over and over in the syrup. Lift out of pan with a perforated spoon and transfer to shallow serving dish.
5.   Add the orange strips to the remaining syrup in the pan. Cook slowly, uncovered, until the peel looks transparent and the syrup is a light gold in colour.
6.   Strain the hot syrup over the oranges then spoon equal amounts of peel on the top of each. Leave until cold then refrigerate for 3 to 4 hours or until thoroughly chilled. To facilitate eating, serve with knives and forks.

Avocado Sea Foam — serves 6 generously

> *finely grated peel of 1 well-washed and dried lime*
> *juice of 2 limes*
> *juice of 1 medium lemon*
> *2 large avocados*
> *3 level tablespoons caster sugar*
> *1 carton (150ml/¼ pt) soured cream*

Decoration
about 1 tablespoon very finely chopped pistachio nuts (blanched first)
fresh mint leaves

1. Mix the grated peel with the juices of the limes and lemon.
2. Peel the avocados as you would peel an ordinary pear, starting at the pointed end. Dice the flesh. Blend until smooth and paste-like in a blender goblet.
3. Spoon into a bowl. Add the citrus mixture. Beat until smooth. Fold in the sugar and soured cream. When the mixture is smooth and evenly combined, cover and refrigerate for 1 hour.
4. To serve, swirl attractively into 6 glass dishes. Sprinkle with pistachios then decorate with clusters of mint leaves.

Danish Apple 'Cake' — serves about 4

> *¾kg (1½ lb) cooking apples*
> *3 tablespoons water*
> *150ml (5 oz) granulated sugar*
> *75g (3 oz) butter*
> *75g (3 oz) fresh white breadcrumbs*
> *50g (2 oz) soft brown sugar (light variety)*
> *1 level teaspoon cinnamon (optional)*
> *150ml (¼ pt) double cream*
> *1 tablespoon milk*
> *1 level tablespoon caster sugar*
> *plum jam for decoration*

1. Peel and core the apples. Cut into thin slices. Put into a pan with water. Cook slowly, covered, until the apples are very soft and pulpy.
2. Beat to a light snow. Add the granulated sugar. Stand over a low heat until dissolved, stirring to prevent sticking. Leave on one side until cold.
3. Heat the butter in a frying pan. As soon as it begins to sizzle, add the crumbs, sugar and cinnamon. Fry gently, turning and stirring all the time, until the mixture is crisp and golden. Allow about 7 minutes.
4. Tip the crumb mixture into a basin and leave until completely cold. To put the 'cake' together, fill 4 tubby tumblers with alternate layers of apple and breadcrumb mixture, finishing with crumbs and leaving a gap of about 2½cm (1 in) at the top of each glass.
5. To decorate, beat the cream, milk and caster sugar together until thick. Pile over the top layer of the crumb mixture in the glasses. Decorate each with blobs of jam.

Peasant Girl with Veil — serves 4

This is another typically Danish speciality and is a variation of the above.

To make, use crumbs made from Danish rye bread instead of white bread. Cover every apple layer *thinly* with melted plum jam. Decorate in the same way as the Danish Apple 'Cake'.

Chilled Orange Cheesecake — serves 6 to 8

Base
125g (4 oz) digestive biscuits, crushed
25g (1 oz) caster sugar
50g (2 oz) butter, melted

Filling
1 packet (225g/8 oz) Philadelphia cream cheese
2 level teaspoons finely grated orange peel
1 teaspoon lemon juice
50g (2 oz) caster sugar
2 large eggs, separated
15g (½ oz) gelatine
3 tablespoons water

1. Brush a 20cm (8 in) loose-bottomed cake tin with melted butter. To make the base, mix the biscuits with sugar and butter. Sprinkle thickly over the base of the tin. Leave on one side temporarily.
2. For the filling, beat the cheese with the orange peel, lemon juice, sugar and egg yolks.
3. Soften the gelatine in 2 tablespoons water for 5 minutes. Transfer to a small pan. Add the rest of the water. Stir over a low heat until dissolved. Cool. Whisk gently into the cheese mixture.
4. Whisk the egg whites to a stiff snow. Fold into the cheese mixture with a large metal spoon. Pour into the tin over the crumbs. Chill in the refrigerator for about 4 hours or until firm and set. Cut into wedges with a knife dipped in cold water.

Fruit-Topped Cheesecake — serves 6 to 8

Make exactly as above. Just before serving, top with fresh sliced strawberries, crushed raspberries or well-drained canned peach slices.

Apricot and Advocaat Cream with Almonds — serves 6

1 can (about ½kg/1 lb) apricots
2 tablespoons brandy
275ml (½ pt) double cream
2 tablespoons milk
4 tablespoons advocaat
25g (1 oz) blanched and split almonds, toasted

1.   Drain the apricots. (Reserve syrup and use in fruit salads or, with soda water, as a base for cold drinks.) Divide the fruit equally between 6 dishes. Sprinkle brandy over each.
2.   Beat the cream and milk together until softly stiff. Fold in advocaat then spoon over the fruit in the dishes.
3.   Sprinkle with almonds and refrigerate for about 2 hours before serving.

Sumptuous Cheesecake — serves 10

> *125g (4 oz) chocolate digestive biscuits, finely crushed*
> *¾kg (1½ lb) (3 large packets) Philadelphia cream cheese*
> *125g (4 oz) butter, melted*
> *3 standard (grade 3) eggs*
> *finely grated peel and juice of 1 well-washed and dried lemon*
> *1 level tablespoon cornflour*
> *1 teaspoon vanilla essence*
> *125g (4 oz) caster sugar*

1.   Brush a 20cm (8 in) spring pan form (a cake tin with clip on sides) with melted butter. Cover the base thickly with crumbs. Set oven to cool, 150°C/300°F, Gas 3.
2.   Place the cheese in a bowl. Beat in all the remaining ingredients, and continue beating until the mixture is absolutely smooth and ultra creamy. If preferred, use a food processor or blender.
3.   Pour into the prepared tin over the crushed biscuits. Bake in the oven for about 1 to 1½ hours or until the filling is set like a baked egg custard. To test, gently insert a cocktail stick into the centre of the cake. If it comes out clean with no uncooked pieces of mixture clinging to it, the cheesecake is ready.
4.   Cool to lukewarm in the oven with the door open and the heat switched off. Remove from the oven, leave until completely cold then refrigerate for several hours when the cheesecake should be firm. Cut into wedges to serve.

Soured Cream Topped Cheesecake — serves 10

When the cake is cooked, remove from the oven and cover the top with 1 carton (150ml/¼ pt) soured cream. Cool off in the oven as described above.

Soured Cream Cheesecake with Pistachios — serves 10

Make exactly as Soured Cream Topped Cheesecake above, but sprinkle with finely chopped, blanched pistachio nuts after removing from the oven.

Kiwi Pavlova — serves 8 to 10

> *4 egg whites*

½ level teaspoon cream of tartar
275g (10 oz) caster sugar
2 level teaspoons cornflour
1 teaspoon vinegar
1 teaspoon vanilla essence

Topping
275ml (½ pt) double cream
2 tablespoons milk
2 tablespoons caster sugar
4 Kiwi fruits, peeled and sliced

1.   Line a large oiled tray with either non-stick parchment paper or 2 layers of greaseproof paper. *Do not* oil the paper. Outline a 22½cm (9 in) circle on paper.
2.   Put the egg whites and cream of tartar into a clean, dry bowl. Beat until very stiff, allowing about 5 to 7 minutes with electric beaters and at least 10 minutes by hand.
3.   Add a third of the sugar. Continue to whisk until the meringue is extra stiff and shiny and stands in high, firm peaks when the beaters are lifted out of the bowl.
4.   Whisk in next third of the sugar gently. Lastly, fold in the remaining sugar with cornflour, vinegar and essence.
5.   Pile the mixture on to the paper, completely filling in the marked circle and swirling the meringue to form ripples. *Do not* smooth it. Bake for 1½ hours in a cool oven set to 120°C/250°F, Gas ½.
6.   Cool slightly. Invert on to a platter, removing the paper. Leave until completely cold. Before serving, whip the cream until thick with the milk and sugar. Pile over the Pavlova then decorate with slices of Kiwi fruit.

Exotic Pavlova — serves 8 to 10

Make exactly as above. Instead of Kiwi fruit, decorate the top with the following canned and drained fruits: lychees, paw-paw, mango slices and cut-up guavas.

Strawberries Romanoff — serves 8

1kg (2 lb) fresh strawberries
150ml (¼ pt) Curaçao
275ml (½ pt) double cream
75g (3 oz) caster sugar
extra strawberries for decoration

1.   Wash and hull the strawberries. Carefully dry. Slice. Place in a bowl and toss with the Curaçao. Cover. Refrigerate for 2 hours.

2.   When ready to serve, spoon equal amounts of the fruit and liqueur into 8 wine-type glasses.

3.   Whip the cream and sugar together until softly stiff. Pile over the strawberries in dishes. Decorate with extra strawberries and serve straight away.

Kissel — serves 8

1¼l (2 pt) strained fruit juice made from stewing a mixture of currants and black-
berries (unsweetened)
225g (8 oz) caster sugar
finely grated peel of 1 small lemon
75g (3 oz) potato flour or cornflour
275ml (½ pt) cold water
extra sugar for sprinkling over the top
about 150ml (¼ pt) single cream

1.   Pour the fruit juice into a saucepan. Add sugar. Stir over low heat until dissolved. Sprinkle in the peel.

2.   Mix potato flour or cornflour to a smooth liquid — gradually — with the cold water. Add to the fruit juice and sugar in the pan.

3.   Slowly bring to the boil, stirring non-stop. When the mixture has cleared and thickened, remove from the heat and pour into 8 small dishes. Sprinkle with extra sugar to prevent a skin from forming. Cool. Chill for a few hours in the refrigerator.

4.   Before serving, float single cream over each.

Note
This is a well-beloved fruit dish both in northern Europe and Russia. It has a delicious flavour and resembles a lightly set fruit blancmange.

Wine Jelly — serves 8

6 level teaspoons gelatine
150ml (¼ pt) cold water

1 bottle (1 litre/1¾ pt) dry red wine
strips of peel cut from 1 small lemon
3 cloves
1 small blade mace
5cm (2 in) piece of cinnamon stick
caster sugar to taste

} tied together in piece of clean cloth

Topping
150ml (¼ pt) whipped cream, lightly sweetened

1. Soften the gelatine in cold water for 5 minutes. Leave on one side temporarily.
2. Meanwhile, pour the wine into a saucepan. Add the lemon peel and the bag of spices. Bring slowly to the boil. Lower the heat. Add sugar to taste. Stir over a moderate heat until dissolved.
3. Move the pan to one side. Cover. Leave to stand until the wine is lukewarm. Strain. Return to a clean pan. Add the softened gelatine and stir over a low heat until dissolved. *Do not* allow the mixture to boil.
4. Pour into 8 dishes and chill in the refrigerator until lightly set (or firmly, depending on taste). Top each with cream before serving.

Mocha Hazelnut Mousse -- serves 4

125g (4 oz) plain chocolate
15g (½ oz) butter
2 level teaspoons instant coffee powder
1 tablespoon Kahlua or Tia Maria
4 standard (grade 3) eggs, separated

Decoration
1 tablespoon hazelnuts, finely chopped

1. Break up the chocolate and put into basin standing over a saucepan of gently simmering water. Add the butter, coffee powder and liqueur.
2. Leave until the chocolate has melted, stirring occasionally. Remove the basin from the pan of water and wipe dry. Beat the egg yolks into the chocolate mixture. Leave on one side temporarily.
3. Beat the egg whites to a stiff snow. Fold smoothly and evenly into chocolate etc, using a large metal spoon.
4. Spoon into 4 glass dishes and refrigerate overnight or for several hours during the day. Just before serving, sprinkle liberally with the nuts.

Gooseberry and Rhubarb Chiffon — serves 6

225g (8 oz) gooseberries, tipped and tailed
225g (8 oz) rhubarb (trimmed weight), cut into 2½cm (1 in) pieces

3 tablespoons water
125g (4 to 5 oz) caster sugar
2 level teaspoons powdered gelatine softened in 5 tablespoons cold water
3 standard (grade 3) eggs, separated
2 level teaspoons finely grated orange peel
red food colouring

1. Place the gooseberries into a saucepan with the rhubarb. Add water. Slowly bring to the boil. Cover the pan. Lower the heat. Cook gently until the fruits are very soft and pulpy.
2. Add sugar and stir until dissolved. Blend to a smooth purée in a blender goblet. Return to a low heat. Add the softened gelatine. Stir until melted. Remove from the heat. Cool to lukewarm. Beat in the egg yolks.
3. Spoon the mixture into a dish and leave until completely cold. Transfer to the refrigerator and leave until the fruit mixture is just beginning to thicken and set.
4. Stir in the orange peel then fold in the egg whites, first beaten to a stiff and peaky snow. Add a few drops of red colouring to brighten the mixture. Continue to fold and stir until smooth.
5. Transfer to 6 glass dishes and leave in the refrigerator until firm and set. If liked, serve with cream.

Fluffy Chocolate and Coffee Whip — serves 4 to 5

575ml (1 pt) milk
50g (2 oz) plain chocolate
1 level tablespoon cocoa powder, sifted
3 level teaspoons instant coffee powder
50g (2 oz) fine semolina
50g (2 oz) caster sugar
2 standard eggs, separated

1. Place the first 5 ingredients into a heavy-based saucepan. Stir over *minimal* heat until the chocolate melts.
2. Increase the heat slightly and cook, stirring continuously, until mixture comes to the boil and thickens. Add the sugar and stir until dissolved. Remove from the heat.
3. Beat in the egg yolks. Whisk the egg whites to a stiff snow. Using a large metal spoon, fold into the chocolate semolina mixture.
4. When well-combined and smooth, spoon the mixture into 4 glasses. Leave plain or decorate with mounds of whipped cream and trickles of Tia Maria.

Lemon and Orange Sherry Syllabub — serves 6

150ml (¼ pt) sweet sherry

finely grated peel and juice of 1 medium lemon
finely grated peel of 1 small orange
50g (2 oz) caster sugar
275ml (½ pt) double cream

Decoration
fresh mint leaves

1. In a large bowl, combine the sherry, lemon peel and juice, orange peel and sugar. Cover. Refrigerate for about 5 hours.
2. Gradually add the cream then beat steadily until the mixture thickens and stands in soft peaks when the beaters are lifted out of the bowl.
3. Spoon neatly into 6 wine-type glasses and refrigerate for between 4 and 6 hours before serving. Decorate with mint leaves at the last minute.

Strawberry Chantilly Apples — serves 6

1kg (2 lb) cooking apples
4 tablespoons water
5 level tablespoons caster sugar
4 rounded tablespoons whole fruit strawberry jam
1 level teaspoon finely grated lemon peel
275ml (½ pt) double cream
2 tablespoons milk

Decoration
extra strawberry jam

1. Peel, core and thinly slice the apples. Place in a saucepan with water. Cook, covered, until the apples are very soft and pulpy. Either whip to a purée or blend until smooth in a blender goblet.
2. Return to the pan, add sugar and stir over a low heat until dissolved. Add the jam and lemon peel. Mix well. Leave until cold.
3. Whip the cream and milk together until thick. Fold into the cold apple mixture. Spoon neatly into 6 sundae glasses and decorate each with jam. Chill lightly in the refrigerator before serving.

Chestnut Gin Cream — serves 6

275ml (½ pt) double cream
3 level tablespoons caster sugar
2 tablespoons gin
1 teaspoon vanilla essence
1 can chestnuts in water (275g/10 oz drained weight)
1 medium flake bar, crushed (or 25g/1 oz grated chocolate)

1. Place the first 4 ingredients into a bowl. Whip steadily until thick.

2. Break up the drained chestnuts into smallish pieces. Fold gently into the cream with a large metal spoon.

3. Spoon equal amounts into 6 glass dishes. Top each with the crushed flake bar or grated chocolate. Chill for about 1 hour in the refrigerator before serving.

Date Cream with Grand Marnier — serves 4

350g (12 oz) fresh dates, skinned and stoned
2 tablespoons Grand Marnier
2 tablespoons lemon juice
275ml (½ pt) double cream
1 level tablespoon caster sugar
1 level teaspoon finely grated orange peel

Decoration
12 walnut halves

1. Chop the dates fairly finely and mix with the Grand Marnier and lemon juice.

2. Whip the cream, sugar and orange peel together until softly stiff. Fold in the date mixture with a large metal spoon.

3. Divide equally between 4 glass dishes and top each with 3 walnut halves.

Tutti-Frutti Pineapple — serves 6 to 8

1 medium sized, ripe pineapple
275ml (½ pt) double cream
1 tablespoon milk
4 tablespoons raspberry or loganberry jam

Decoration
50g (2 oz) split and toasted almonds

1. Halve the pineapple lengthwise but *do not* remove the leafy crown; in fact slice straight through it.

2. Remove the centre hard 'core' with a sharp knife. Discard if it is very tough and inedible; otherwise eat up as a snack! *Carefully* cut the flesh out of pineapple halves, taking care not to pierce the skin. However, as a precaution against juices leaking out, line neatly the insides of both halves with foil.

3. Beat the cream and milk together until thick. Fold in the jam and the cut-up pineapple flesh. Return to the pineapple halves. Sprinkle with almonds. Chill lightly before serving.

Apple and Gooseberry Cider Fool — serves 4 to 5

225g (8 oz) cooking apples
225g (8 oz) gooseberries
3 tablespoons sweet cider
4 level tablespoons caster sugar
275ml (½ pt) double cream
red food colouring

1.   Peel, core and slice the apples. Top and tail the gooseberries. Put both the fruits into a pan with the cider.
2.   Bring to the boil, lower the heat and cover. Simmer for 15 to 20 minutes or until the fruit has cooked down to a very soft pulp. Blend, with sugar, to a smooth purée in a blender goblet.
3.   Leave the fruit until completely cold. Whip the cream until stiff then gently fold in the fruit purée. When smooth and evenly combined, heighten the colour by stirring in a few drops of colouring.
4.   Spoon into 4 or 5 glass dishes and chill lightly before serving. If liked, top with some extra whipped cream.

Gooseberry and Raspberry Swirl — serves 4 to 5

Make exactly as the Apple and Gooseberry Cider Fool above but use *only* topped and tailed gooseberries and substitute water for the cider. Add 1 level teaspoon finely grated lemon peel to the fruit while it is cooking. After folding the cold gooseberry purée into the whipped cream, ripple in 125g (4 oz) crushed raspberries sweetened to taste with sifted icing sugar. Spoon into glass dishes and chill lightly before serving.

Chocolate Lime Swirl — serves 6

575ml (1 pt) double cream
75g (3 oz) caster sugar
4 tablespoons lime cordial
125g (4 oz) plain chocolate, melted and cooled

1.   Whip the cream and sugar together until softly stiff. Gently whisk in the lime cordial.
2.   Using a large metal spoon, swirl in the melted chocolate. Spoon into 6 stemmed glasses. Chill lightly before serving with sponge finger biscuits.

Father Christmas Sundaes — serves 6 to 8

4 medium pomegranates
275ml (½ pt) double cream

150ml (¼ pt) single cream
3 level tablespoons caster sugar
2 tablespoons Cherry Brandy

1.   Prepare the pomegranates by cutting each fruit into quarters. Bend the quarters backwards over a bowl. The seeds, with a bit of help from your fingers, will come away from the skin etc very easily.
2.   In a separate bowl, beat both the creams and the sugar together until softly stiff. Gently beat in the Cherry Brandy and continue beating until the cream is stiff.
3.   Slowly stir in the pomegranate seeds and divide mixture equally between 6 or 8 glass dishes. Refrigerate lightly before serving.
Note
If liked, decorate with small holly leaves made from almond paste, tinted green.

Peach Foam 'Melba' — serves 6 to 8

1 packet lemon or orange flavour jelly
cold water
3 large peaches, blanched as tomatoes and then skinned
2 teaspoons lemon juice
150ml (¼ pt) double cream
2 egg whites

Sauce
225g (8 oz) fresh raspberries
50g (2 oz) caster sugar
1 tablespoon kirsch

1.   Make up the packet jelly to 275ml (½ pt) with water. Tip into a pan. Stir over a low heat until the jelly dissolves.
2.   Halve the peaches then cut directly into a blender goblet. Add the lemon juice. Blend until smooth. Stir into the jelly.
3.   Beat the cream until thick. Fold into the peach mixture with a large metal spoon. When smooth and evenly combined, cover and leave in the cool until just beginning to thicken and set.
4.   Beat the egg whites to a stiff snow. Whisk the jelly mixture until foamy. Fold the whites into the jelly foam with a metal spoon. Refrigerate until just on the point of setting.
5.   Spoon into 6 or 8 dishes and refrigerate until set. Just before serving, blend the raspberries to a smooth purée with the sugar and kirsch, then spoon equal amounts over each portion of peach foam.

Peach and Whisky Almond Ice — serves about 8

275ml (½ pt) double cream
1 tablespoon cold milk
4 level tablespoons caster sugar
1 egg white, stiffly whisked
1 tablespoon whisky
25g (1 oz) flaked and toasted almonds
4 large peaches, blanched as tomatoes and then skinned and diced
1 tablespoon lemon juice

1.   Beat the cream and milk together until thick. Fold in the sugar, egg white, whisky and almonds.
2.   Toss the peaches in lemon juice then gently stir into the cream mixture. Spoon into a basin and cover securely with cling film. Freeze for 1½ hours.
3.   Stir round fairly briskly to break down the ice crystals. Cover again and freeze until firm — about 6 to 8 hours.
Note
This ice cream is especially delicious if each portion is coated with strawberry purée, made by crushing 225g (8 oz) fresh strawberries in a blender goblet and sweetening to taste.

Flamingo Peaches Campari — serves 4

140g (4½ oz) caster sugar
9 tablespoons water
4 tablespoons grenadine syrup
2 tablespoons Campari
4 large peaches, blanched as tomatoes then skinned and halved

1.   Place the first 4 ingredients in a pan. Stir over a low heat until the sugar dissolves. Bring to the boil. Boil for 2 minutes.
2.   Pour into bowl (*not* crystal or it will crack). Add the peach halves. Baste with the syrup. Cover the bowl. Leave until completely cold.
3.   Refrigerate for a minimum of 3 hours, stirring the peaches round in the syrup about every hour.
4.   Serve with raspberry, lemon or orange sorbet.

Sample Menus

Lunch Menus

Dressed Mushrooms
Pancakes Neapolitan
Leaf spinach
Zabaglione with Brandied Peaches

* * * * * * * * *

Palm Heart & Brazil Nut Cocktail
Gratin Dauphinoise
Cauliflower & Green Pepper Salad
Chestnut Gin Cream

* * * * * * * * *

Chilled Tomato Consommé with Drambuie
Macaroni in Blue Cheese Cream Sauce
Finnish Pineapple Salad
Honey & Banana Pudding with Rum Cream

* * * * * * * * *

Courtly Cream of Mustard Soup
Avocado Mousse
Paradise Salad
Old-Fashioned Syrup Tart

* * * * * * * * *

Artichokes with Tangy Tomato Mayonnaise
Spaghetti with Mushroom & Olive Sauce
Broad Bean Salad
Flamingo Peaches Campari

* * * * * * * * *

Farmhouse Split Pea Soup
Devilled Buck Rarebits
Tomatoes with Creamed Chive Dressing
Date Cream with Grand Marnier

* * * * * * * * *

Dinner Menus

Turnip Cream Soup
Chilli Beans & Chick Peas with Lettuce Cream
Sunshine Salad
Kiwi Pavlova

* * * * * * * * *

Heavenly Cocktail
Mixed Vegetables and Coconut Curry with Yogurt
Autumn Fruit Salad with Mead

* * * * * * * * *

Gingered Ogen Melons
Florence Fennel in Cheesey Pernod Sauce
Butter-Tossed Baby Carrots
Mocha Hazelnut Mousse

* * * * * * * * *

Pineapple & Pomegranate Cocktails
Cheese 'Escalopes'
Sauté Potatoes
Wine Jelly

* * * * * * * * *

Italian 'Lace' Soup
Rice-Stuffed Peppers with Cheese & Walnuts
Avocado Sea Foam

* * * * * * * * *

Chilled Beetroot Soup
Balkan Creamed Egg and Potato Bake
Brussels Sprouts or Cabbage
Sumptuous Cheesecake

* * * * * * * * *

Aubergine Cream Dip
Stir-Fried Almond Rice
Fruit & Nut Orange Pudding

* * * * * * * * *

US/UK Conversion Guide

Spoons
1 US teaspoon or tablespoon = 4/5 equivalent standard UK measure
16 US tablespoons = 1 US cup

Liquid Measures

	US	UK
1 cup	225ml (8 fl oz)	300ml (10 fl oz)
1 pint	450ml (16 fl oz)	600ml (20 fl oz)

In the US dry foods, such as flour, sugar and shortening are usually measured by volume. If a recipe calls for ½ cup, pour the ingredient into a measuring cup up to the 4-oz mark, making sure that it is level.
In the UK dry foods are measured by weight. The following weights of common ingredients all equal 1 US cup.

Breadcrumbs	(fresh	50g (2 oz)
	(dried)	100g (4 oz)
Butter		225g (8 oz)
Dried Fruit	(generous cup)	175g (6 oz)
Flour		100g (4 oz)
Honey	(generous cup)	350g (12 oz)
Rice	(uncooked)	200g (7 oz)
Sugar	(granulated/caster)	225g (8 oz)
	(confectioner's/icing)	100g (4 oz)

Index